W9-DGI-327

THE MYTHIC WORLD
OF THE ZUNI

The Mythic World of the Zuni

As Written by
Frank Hamilton Cushing

Edited and Illustrated
by Barton Wright

University of New Mexico Press
Albuquerque

Library of Congress Cataloging in Publication Data

Cushing, Frank Hamilton, 1857-1900

    The mythic world of the Zuni/as written by Frank Hamilton
Cushing; edited and illustrated by Barton Wright.

        p.cm

    Bibliography; p

    ISBN 0-8263-1387-6

    1. Zuni Indians—Religion and mythology. 2. Indians of North
American—New Mexico—Religion and mythology. I. Wright, Barton,
II. Title.

E99.Z9C892   1988   87-22902

299'.78—dc19   CIP

Contents

Preface

Z uni Pueblo is a small scattered village high up in the plateau country along the western margin of New Mexico. Located about thirty miles south of the railroad town of Gallup, it is most noted today for the skill of its inhabitants in making inlaid silver jewelry and for the dramatic ceremony of the Shalako. This Indian pueblo, lying in the small valley of the Zuni River which is tributary to the Little Colorado, is one of the oldest farming communities in the United States, having been occupied for several centuries before the arrival of the Spanish. There is much more, however, that distinguishes the Zuni Indians.

When the Spanish entered the Southwest before the middle of the sixteenth century, over eighty pueblos were clustered along the Rio Grande and its tributaries. In addition, to the far west were the Hopi towns, then to the east of them the seven Zuni villages and the sky city of Acoma. Six different languages were spoken in the pueblos, Keresan, Tiwa, Tewa, Towa, Shoshonean, and the unique Zunian. Although not of immediate kinship, the pueblos are culturally related. Each town, based on land which it had occupied and used for centuries, was an autonomous unit with its own system of government—both secular and religious. Of all of these people, Zuni had the dubious distinction of being the first pueblo encountered by the Europeans and consequently exposed for the longest time to the devastating Spanish occupation of the Southwest.

The first to arrive in 1539 was a Franciscan Father, Fray Marcos de Niza and his Moorish companion Estevan, who had walked across the width of North America with Cabeza de Vaca. On this journey, Estevan and Cabeza de Vaca had heard tales of the seven great cities of Cibola from the natives they had encountered and now de Niza and Estevan followed the rumors northward seeking the seven great cities of gold. Approaching from the south the first "city" they beheld, its plastered walls lit by the sun, was the ancient Zuni town of Háwikuh, appearing far different from the rancherias to the south. Estevan, secure in his knowledge of the ways of the Indian people, went forward to the village and his subsequent death. Fray Marcos de Niza, who tarried some distance behind, fled south to Mexico with the news of Estevan's death, telling imaginative tales of a golden city seen only through eyes blinded by desire. Enthralled by these stories, Francisco Vasquez de Coronado set forth to find the Golden Cities of Cibola. He reached Zuni in the year of 1540 and the turmoil began.

Driven by the search for gold and souls to save, Zuni was visited by a succession of explorers. Captain Francisco Sanchez Chamuscado arrived in 1581 and was followed by Antonio de Espejo in 1583. In 1598 and again in 1604–05 Juan de Oñate passed through going westward and returning. By 1629 Spanish missionaries had settled into Háwikuh and a Catholic mission rose in its midst. But assimilation was not easy and Spanish efforts were marked by rebellion and martyred priests. In 1680 the Zuni joined in a pueblo-wide revolt, killing one of their priests and burning the mission at Halóna before fleeing their villages for the single fortified town atop the massive nearby mesa of Dówa Yálanne. When the Zuni descended to the valley after the Spanish Reconquest of New Mexico, they settled in a single village in the area of Halóna as a safeguard against the increasing raids of the Apache and Navajo.

From the time of the Reconquest in 1692 and the remaining years of Spanish dominance, through the short period of Mexican rule from 1821 to 1848, and into the interval of explorations by the United States, the Zuni maintained a peaceful relationship. In these later years they served increasingly as a friendly stop, furnishing guides and other services to various expeditions and travelers. Despite this, little was known of Zuni in the mid-nineteenth century and it was only through the work of a few dedicated individuals that the present body of knowledge about the early Zuni was accumulated.

The exploration of the Colorado River system, authorized by the United States Congress in 1869, had been vigorously pursued by Major John Wesley Powell for nearly a decade under various entitlements. While his primary concern was geology, his interest in the Indians of the area was roused. Powell believed that they could not be fully understood without a thorough knowledge of their language. In 1879, when the explorations were discontinued, the United States Geological Survey was created. A separate entity, the Bureau of American Ethnology, was established as part of the Smithsonian Institution to accomodate all anthropological research. It was designed as a service department to collect linguistic and other data of value for use in the administration of Indian affairs. Its directives were to support research among the Indians through the direct employment of scholars and to initiate and guide research by collaborators. One of the first projects was a collecting trip among the Pueblo peoples of the Southwest to be led by "Colonel" James Stevenson. A young curator of ethnography, Frank Hamilton Cushing, was appointed by the secretary of the Smithsonian, Spencer F. Baird, to accompany the expedition. Cushing was instructed to choose his own study area among the Pueblos and select his own methods of study. He chose Zuni.

Frank Hamilton Cushing from his birth through the forty-two productive years of his short life was an anomalous individual. Born in 1857 in Eire County, Pennsylvania, he weighed a mere pound and a half and surprised his physician father by surviving. Later the family moved to Barre Center, New York, where Cushing's early life was shaped by his delicate health and by an unconventional father who believed only in the logical mind and its ability to reason and cared not a fig for the opinion of others. Undoubtedly these beliefs fell on the willing ears of a child who was confined to a bed, unable to exercise for a large part of the time.

That Cushing was a near genius is evidenced by the creativity of his thinking. Yet in many ways it was an undisciplined brilliance that left too many projects incomplete. Unable to compete with his healthy brothers and sister during his formative years, he was seldom to be found in school but rather roamed about the countryside alone when not confined by ill health. The woods and the fields became his school and developed his interest in natural history. His discovery of scattered Indian artifacts in the woods near his home led to his reconstruction of Indian life in his imagination. Cushing reasoned out the uses of many of the Indian tools and utensils and spent countless hours duplicating them. His outstanding ability as a craftsman and his intuitive grasp of the native mind were attested to by all who knew him. His unique childhood led to a firmly entrenched belief that he could pursue any and all interests on his own terms. Despite the eccentricity of this early training, it prepared him admirably well for the major event of his life.

At seventeen he wrote and submitted a paper to the Smithsonian which was very favorably received and published in the Annual Report of 1874. It was on the basis of this paper that Major Powell asked Cushing to join the staff of the Smithsonian as an assistant curator of ethnology in 1875. The following year his capabilities were further recognized by placing him in charge of the National History Museum exhibit for the Philadelphia Centennial. It was during the preparation of this exhibit that he first learned of the Pueblo Indians.

Cushing accompanied Stevenson's expedition by train to Las Vegas, New Mexico, then the terminus of the railroad. From this point the party continued on by wagon and muleback to Ft. Wingate near present day Gallup, a journey of ten days. From there it was a short trip over the mountains to Zuni. Cushing, typically, left the main party and pushed on far ahead of the others to reach Zuni first. Stevenson, on his arrival, set up the main camp in the yard of a missionary, Dr. Ealy, about one quarter of a mile north of the pueblo. Here Hillers, the photographer for the Expedition, and Cushing shared a tent. Arrangements were soon made for Stevenson and his wife to use two of the missionary's back rooms for trading and packing the materials they collected. Stevenson also secured a large room in the Zuni governor's house for Hillers to work. Cushing busied himself about the pueblo making sketches, taking notes, and learning Zuni words.

The original plan had been for Cushing to remain at Zuni for three months, from September through November, but at the end of a month he had not made the progress he desired and had written Baird asking for an extension. Obviously frustrated by living outside of Zuni, he decided to move into the village. Without securing permission from anyone, he simply moved all of his belongings into the governor's house. Whether he was moving into the room used by Hillers or another is not known, but it caused the governor of Zuni and Cushing's companions great consternation. The Zuni viewed his note taking and constant sketching with great suspicion and often outright hostility, so much so that when Cushing moved into the governor's house, someone from that household slept at his doorway to protect him for many months.

Cushing realized that unless he could overcome the suspicions of the Zuni he would never learn anything of importance about their inner life so he concluded to spend more time at Zuni while Stevenson went on to the Hopi. When the party returned at the end of a month and a half, he would rejoin them. This was looked upon with great disfavor by the remainder of the Expedition, although how he was expected to spend three months at Zuni without remaining behind is unclear. In addition to his poor status among the Zuni he was not on good terms with Dr. Ealy, the missionary, and Graham, the trader to whom he might have turned, was absent. Nevertheless Cushing persevered, but he watched the preparations for the departure of the Expedition the next morning with trepidation. This feeling was well justified for in the morning at sunrise when he went to bid them goodbye they had left without a word. Furthermore, the supplies that were supposed to have been left for Cushing had been claimed by the missionary, who would give him nothing. It was a despairing Cushing, with neither food nor shelter of his own, who was forced to throw himself upon the mercy of the Zuni.

When Stevenson returned in mid-November from the Hopi villages, he brought with him the extension which Cushing had requested. What had begun as a three-month stay stretched on for four and a half years. During this time he became even further estranged from his white neighbors, who regarded him with all of the opprobrium reserved for a "squaw man" in that era of Indian prejudice, and even more deeply committed to the Zuni.

Cushing's single-minded, egocentric determination to pursue his own course of research had undoubtedly set him at cross purposes with the Stevensons and others. Matilda Coxe Stevenson believed in examining the Zuni like recalcitrant children and, if the need arose, bribing or bullying them to get the desired information. Cushing, on the other hand, tried to become Indian in thought and behavior, becoming the first scientific participant observer whether intentionally or not. The two detested one another and the method each used (Cushing 1979, 24–5).

Matilda Stevenson's notes, combined with those of her husband, produced a descriptive treatise consistent with the state of the technical approach of her time. Cushing, however, not only recorded similar material but conveyed the feeling and depth of the source from which it sprang. His information was not presented in the tidy fashion of Mrs. Stevenson but instead emerged in spurts, often incomplete in coverage. Most of his writings are buried in little known publications of limited circulation as articles. He produced no major book in his life time. The work he is most noted for, *Zuni Tales* (1901), was published by his wife after his death. Cushing's information on Zuni corn, its origin, care, and preparation, appeared in a series of articles in *The Millstone* (Vols. 9–10, Jan. 1884–Aug. 1885). This material was titled *Zuni Breadstuff* and was reprinted by the Museum of the American Indian in 1920 and again in 1974. Insights into his relationship with the Zuni may be gleaned from his article, *My Adventures in Zuni*, first printed in *Century Illustrated Magazine* (Vols. XXV and XXVI, 1882–83) and later reprinted by Filter Press (1967) and again by Northland Press in 1970. However, the most informative book on Cushing both as a person and a scholar is Jesse Green's *Zuni; Selected Writings of Frank Hamilton Cushing* (Cushing 1979). Green's commentaries present Cushing's difficulties with his peers and superiors, and with his health, but more importantly focus on his many contributions to natural history and its related fields.

Decades ahead of his time in anthropological method, Cushing influenced both European and American thought, but more importantly he gave us a brief glimpse of Zuni life through the eyes of a native.

Introduction

One of the richest legacies of the first inhabitants of America to the cultural fabric of our society is their oral tradition. Within this tradition are myths and legends that explain their worlds, enhance their ceremonies, entertain and amuse them, and interweave many disparate people with common themes. Native American stories have fired our imaginations and infiltrated our literature for generations until today it is as common to know a Coyote story as it is to know one from Uncle Remus.

In the Southwest these tales run the gamut from fables that rival those of Aesop to the bedtime stories told by a grandmother from anywhere in the world. There are fairy tales, ghost stories, imaginary epics, all designed to amuse or present a moral lesson. There are also odysseys that encapsulate generations of shifting occupation, migrations, strangers encountered who must either become friends or be fought as bitter enemies. There are tales of threatening natural disasters overcome, of families and individuals dislocated or divided into groups. Each story is told with oratorical grandeur or in the romantic nuances of poetry. Every one of these legends bears within it an event of importance that should be remembered by the people. For those without writing, this information can be carried only in the variable minds of men and passed from one to another verbally. Through time the actual event may be enhanced or abridged but, regardless of how faded and worn it becomes, a kernel of truth remains of an important event to be passed on to successive generations so they may know of their own history. Although we pride ourselves on committing similar information to paper to be checked and rechecked for accuracy and stored in some permanent form, our oral traditions continue unabated despite all such technological advances. "Of course Washington threw a silver dollar across the Potomac." Despite the constant debunking of this fable, every school child knows it and it persists, for some of the ingredients are true or desirable. There is a Potomac River and most assuredly there was a man named Washington who lived near it and who performed many great deeds for which he was admired. He was so capable that undoubtedly he could have thrown a silver dollar across the Potomac. In just such a manner native American legends contain an illusive element of truth. Similarly, original thoughts and philosophical concepts on the nature of man and his relationship to the universe and his gods are passed along, often so well integrated into ritual as to be almost unrecognizable.

In the Southwest the early ethnographers avidly collected everything available, from artifacts to folklore. Occasionally the material was wrested from unwilling donors but, despite the injustices that may have occurred, it is to these individuals, both native and non-native, that a debt is owed for the written accounts of many Indian traditions. Obtained before the process of acculturation had begun in earnest to erode the methods of transmission as well as the contents of the message itself, these stories have an inherent integrity. They constitute a frozen moment in the continuum of tradition before the feedback of a hundred years of exposure to ethnographers and their hypotheses and treatises had blurred the boundaries and melded separate folklore identities. Secured long before the warping effect of land claims, legal rights, and disputed beliefs had further clouded contemporary accounts, the first recorded traditions consequently often contain the most cogent legends.

Many other factors also obscure the elements that compose a myth, not the least being the disparity between native imagery and the cultural bias of the recorder. In many instances all of the elements of a myth are not spelled out as they are unnecessary for the native listener who has known such things since childhood. But to the non-native recorder such nuances are often lost. Among the Zuni there is a specific time and place for the telling of these stories, a constraint that dictates what the listener may hear.

It must also be borne in mind that there is no single authoritative mythology. Each myth has countless versions, each varying with the background of the storyteller. The bare bones account of a secular story varies greatly from the sacred which delves deep into details, parading esoteric information, often with repetitious recounting of the theme. The mark of a good raconteur has always been how skillfully he embroiders a tale to make it more interesting and the Zuni are no exception to this, even though the kind of embroidery may be foreign to our ears. With the variations possible through sacred, secular, group, and individual recitals, the theme is often embellished almost beyond recognition, yet, much in the manner of the three blind men examining an elephant, the elements that are necessary to a particular myth may be discovered and examined.

One of the first to study Zuni mythology was Frank Hamilton Cushing. Anthropologically ahead of his time in his role of participant-observer among the Zuni, he learned their language and often understood the unspoken context of the myths and was able to convey this in his writing. Regardless of the enhanced romanticism of his literary work, it provided many excellent insights into the Zuni ethos. From the contemporary vantage point, built upon his and other subsequent works, a few flaws in his efforts may be uncovered that must be taken into consideration for they are not free from the strong cultural bias of the times. But beneath the florid writing filled with quaint turns of phrase and Victorian attitudes, there are solid data supported by subsequent work.

The material presented in the *Outlines of Zuni Creation Myths* appears to be the main body of Cushing's notes on mythology. These notes are referred to as an ongoing project from 1884 until their publication with an interpretive overview of prehistory in 1896. Short articles such as "The Origin of Corn" (*The Millstone* vol. IX, no. 1 1884, 1–3) and other myths appear to have been extracted. In these stories much seems to have been abridged or glossed over by Cushing, undoubtedly to appeal to a specific audience, while in the former they are more complete.

Buried in the Thirteenth Annual Report of the Bureau of American Ethnology (1896), this collection of myths presents Zuni thoughts on the origins of the cosmos, of the deities, the earth, and the all-important food, corn. They explain social organization, the Kachina Cult, and the early wanderings of the Zuni or *Áshiwi* around the Southwest. The stories are too good to be left to chance discovery by a small audience. Retold and illustrated here they are accompanied by additional information retrieved from many and varied sources. It must be recognized that any interpretation of a myth is highly subjective even though there are elements that require closer scrutiny and discussion. There are fragments that should be pulled together to show similarities, or that have supporting data acquired from the fields of art, archaeology, or ethography. The annotations of these legends are not aimed at the solution of problems but rather are explanations, tentative, undoubtedly simplistic, but possibly of interest to others who may also share the enjoyment of these myths.

Genesis

1
Genesis

Before the beginning only the All-Father, Áwonawílona, the Maker and Container of All, had being. Throughout the great space of ages there was nothing else but black darkness and everywhere a desolate and endless void.

Pondering this emptiness and desiring a better condition, the All-Father conceived within himself and projected his thoughts outward in space where the mists of increase, potent steams of growth, were evolved and coalesced. Through his omniscience, the All-Container shaped himself into the person and form of the Sun whom we hold to be our father and who thus came to exist and appear. With his appearance as the Sun came the brightening of the spaces with light and in this luminescence the great mist clouds thickened and fell, growing to become the immense world-holding waters.

From his surface the Sun Father, Yatoka, drew substance to form the seed for two differing worlds and therewith impregnated the great waters. Under the heat of his light, the water grew warm and green. Upon the sea a scum arose, waxing ever greater and dividing until it became Áwitelin

1

Tsíta, the four-fold enclosing Earth Mother and Ápoyan Ta'chu, the all-covering Sky Father lying close together upon the Great Waters

From this lying together the two conceived all of the beings of earth, men and creatures, in the four-fold womb of the world. Growing large with her children, the Earth Mother sank into the embrace of the waters below leaving the Sky Father clasped by the waters above.

Now like all Supernal Beings, the Earth Mother and the Sky Father were amorphous, changeable, even as smoke in the wind, transmutable as thought, capable of manifesting themselves in any form at will, as dancers may with mask making. Thus as man and woman they spoke to one another.

Concerned for the welfare of her burgeoning progeny, the Earth Mother sought to delay their birth while she took counsel with their Sky Father, asking, "How shall our children, when born, know one place from another even by your light?"

2

Earth Mother

2
Formation of the Worlds

Long the two thought and conferred with one another until at last their path was clear. "Behold!" said the Earth Mother, and a great terraced bowl full of water appeared at hand. "This is how the homes of my tiny children shall be upon my body. On the rim of each country they wander in, terraced mountains shall stand, making one space into many different countries and separating one place from another.

"Behold again!" she said, and spat upon the waters which she then smote with her fingers and rapidly stirred. Foam appeared and formed, gathering along the terraced rim and mounting ever higher and higher. "From my bosom they shall take nourishment, for in such as this they will find the substance of life as we were ourselves sustained!" With her warm breath she blew gently across the terraces and white flecks of foam broke away and floated above the water. Whereupon the attending Sky Father blew his cold breath upon them until they scattered, shedding downward a fine mist and spray. "Thus," spoke the Earth Mother, "shall white clouds float up from the Great Waters at the rim of the world, clustering about the mountain terraces until borne aloft and abroad by the breaths of the supernal soul-beings and the children. These will be torn asunder by your cold, shedding downward in rain-spray the water of life into the hollow places of my lap! For there shall our children nestle, both mankind and creature-kind, in search of warmth from your coldness." Even so today the trees on high mountains crouch low toward the Earth Mother for warmth and protection.

"Yet not alone shall you be helpful to our children," spoke the Sky Father, "for behold!" and within the wrinkles and crevices of his hand he placed the semblance of shining yellow corn grains. In the dusk of that early world dawn they gleamed like sparks of fire as, palm downward, he moved his hand across the bowl. From below, shining up from the depths of the water, they also moved following the path of his hand.

"See!" said he, pointing to seven grains clasped by his thumb and four fingers, "By such light shall our children be guided. For when I am not about, and your terraces are as the dark itself, then our children shall be guided by lights like these, from all six regions wheeling around the midmost one, as in and around the center where our children shall abide lie all the other regions of space. Furthermore, just as these grains gleam up from the water, so shall seed-grains like them, yet numberless, spring up from thy bosom when touched by my waters, to nourish our children."

Formation of the Worlds

Twin Children of the Sun

3
Birth of the Twins

Deep in the lowermost womb, in the stygian cave-world of Ánosin Téhuli, the place of first formation, the seed of men and creatures took shape, multiplying in kind and increasing until the space was overfilled. Unfinished beings were everywhere, crawling like reptiles over one another in the filth and darkness of the first world until, like the swollen egg case of some insect, it threatened to burst. So thickly crowded together that they trod upon one another, they lived in mud burrows and ate grass seeds as they slowly grew wiser and more man-like until many sought to escape.

Long and deeply the Sun Father took counsel with himself over the problem of the living creatures as they clamored ever more loudly below, before he came to a decision. Casting his glance about the Great Waters beneath, he searched until he spied a bubble capped with foam floating near the Earth Mother. With a single ray he impregnated it as it nestled there. Nurtured by the Earth Mother's warmth and the soft gentle rain, the cap of foam grew and brought forth twin boys, the Beloved Twain Who

Descended, two brothers, one preceding, the other following, like voice and echo, the elder Ko'wituma, the younger Wats'usi.

To these children the Sun Father imparted much of his sacred knowledge, giving them devices to better perform their duties. In recognition of their origin and close ties to the Earth Mother and himself he gave each a cap patterned after the original cap of foam. With the great cloud bows and flint-tipped arrows he armed the Twins. For protection, he gave each the fog-making shield of netting spun from floating clouds and the wind-driven spray that would both hide and defend. Then, as a man gives control of his work to his two hands, the Sun Father gave his sons dominion or fathership over all men and creatures.

Well instructed by the Sun Father, they lifted him with their great cloud bows into the vault of the zenith so the earth might become warm and thus more fit for their children, men and creatures alike. Then seated upon their shields, the Twin Gods floated swiftly westward seeking the best place to enter the dark netherworld. Grasping their flint-tipped thunderbolts, they selected a place and cleft the land, penetrating to its depths; still seated upon their shields they sank into the blackness of the first Underworld.

Birth of the Twins

Wing World

4
The First World

Now in the gloomy black depths of the first world, Ánosin Téhuli, grasses and crawling vines sprang up below the cleft opened by the Twins, and began growing toward the light as plants are wont to do. Upon reaching the sooty netherworld, the Beloved Twins seized these grasses and breathed upon them whereupon they increased mightily in size. As they grew, the two brothers took firm hold of them and walked about twisting the grasses together and pushing them upward until they reached the dimness of the second cave-world. At each spot where they had grasped the stalks, leaves and stems sprang forth making a great ladder whereupon men and creatures might ascend to the second world. Men and other beings crowded after the Twins in their struggle upward to this new land, K'ólin Téhuli, the Moss World. Not all succeeded and many fell back into the darkness, to become deformed and demoniac, monsters or strange beings who even now escape from the depths when the earth quivers and cracks.

This second world, although as dark as night filled with storm, was yet larger than the first world and here men and creatures could increase without crawling upon one another. But all of the beings began to multiply and soon they filled up the Moss World and once more they clamored for release. The two small but Mighty Ones once again caused the Great Ladder to grow upward and then gathered the beings into groups, guiding each upward toward the increasing light of the third world, Áwisho Téhuli, the World of Mud.

Because they emerged at different times, each successive group varied from the others. This third cave-world was not as dark as the previous worlds. The light was like that of a clear and starry night, yet the people complained of the glare. But even this larger land soon became crowded as all the beings separated and multiplied to become different creatures and tribes. Once more the Two came to guide the ever-increasing hordes upward although many were again lost to the darkness below.

Upon reaching the last cave-world, Tépahaian Téhuli, Wing World, the light was like the gray dawn of morning flaring wing-like across the sky and all hid their eyes from the brightness. As their eyes became accustomed to the light, they stared about and the various beings began to perceive their differences. According to their nature, everyone began to understand somewhat when the Beloved Two sought to instruct them, urging all to seek first the Sun Father who could reveal to them the knowledge and the wisdom of the ways of life.

First Warrior of the Sun

5
The Daylight World

At long last the Two led forth the nations of men and the groups of creatures into the great upper world of the Sun, Ték'ohaian Úlahnane, the Daylight World. The men and creatures that emerged were more like one another than they are now, for our fathers were black like the caves they came from, with cold and scaly skins like other mud creatures. Their eyes bulged and blinked constantly like those of the owl. Their ears were bat-like and their feet and hands were webbed as are those of the ones who walk in wet soft places. All had tails which became longer with age. They crouched and crawled like lizards and toads and moved bent over with the uncertain steps of infants fearful of falling or stumbling in the dim light. Hence it was that the Twins brought forth Mankind late at night so they might be more easily accommodated.

As the great star of morning, Móyachun Thlánna, rose and its light struck their eyes they thought it was the Sun Father, for it burned their weak vision. But it was only the Elder of the Bright Ones who, with his shield of flame, heralded the arrival of the Sun Father.

When the Sun Father did appear, low in the east rising from the Great Waters, they were blinded by his glory and flung themselves on the ground, wallowing in the dirt and covering their eyes with bare arms and hands as they cried out in anguish. Yet like the moth that goes back to the flame even though burned, they looked again and again.

Before long they grew accustomed to the light and rising up, saw the great world they had entered. When they arose and no longer stayed bent and crouched they saw each other as naked. Rushing about they covered themselves with girdles of bark or rushes and wove plaited sandals of yucca fiber for their sore feet.

It was then that men grew to know things and were instructed by what they saw, becoming wiser and more able to receive the words of the Twin Gods, of elder brothers, fathers, and priests. For in each world there had been those who found and cherished things given by the gods, gifts of unknown purpose or function. But in the light of the Sun Father, all became clear. The first and most perfect of these men, Yaná-uluha, brought up water from the Inner Ocean and seeds of growing things as well as other objects of great power.

The Summer and Winter People

6
The Winter and Summer People

The first wise man, Yaná-uluha, came carrying a staff which appeared now in the daylight to be covered with many plumes of striking color—yellow, blue green, red, white, black, and variegated. Attached to the staff were sea shells and other potent things brought from the Underworld. When the people saw this beautiful staff and heard the song-like tinkle of the sacred shells, they stretched forth their hands toward it and cried out like children asking questions.

Yaná-uluha, having been made wise by the masters of life or god beings, replied, "It is a staff to test the hearts and understandings of the children." Balancing it in his hand he struck it on a hard place and blew upon it. Instantly amid the plumes there appeared four round things, the seeds of moving creatures, eggs. Two of these were blue like the sky or turquoise and the other two were a dun red like the flesh of the Earth Mother. Again the people cried out in wonder, asking many questions.

Then Yaná-uluha said, "These are the seeds of living things. From two shall emerge beautiful things with plumage colored like the leaves and shoots of summer plants. Where they fly you must follow, for where they are it will be everlasting summer. You will know neither pain nor toil but will always have fertile fields of food. From the other pair shall come ugly beings, uncolored, black, or piebald. Where they fly you must follow. There winter will contend with summer. You will work hard in the fields and your offspring will compete with those of the birds for the fruit of your labors."

With scarcely a thought, the strongest and hastiest people rushed to take the beautiful blue eggs, leaving the other two for those who cautiously waited. The hasty ones carried the turquoise eggs gently to the warm sands below a cliff and guarded them there, speculating as they waited on the beauty the eggs must contain. At last small beaks emerged through cracks in the shells. Those who had chosen them plied the unseen hatchlings with morsels of their own food to give them strength, thus building the appetites of the little birds for the food of men. But when at last these birds hatched they were black with white bandings, for they were the magpie and the raven, who flew away croaking and mocking our fathers.

The eggs taken by the patient ones who had waited became gorgeous macaws and parrots that Yaná-uluha wafted to the far southland with a toss of his wand. As father, yet child, of the macaw, he chose the symbol and the name for himself and for those who had waited. The macaw and the kindred of the macaw became the Múlakwe, while those who had chosen the magpie and raven became the Ka'kakwe, the Raven People.

Thus were the people divided into the People of Winter and the People of Summer. Those who chose the raven were many, forceful and strong. Those who chose the macaw were fewer in number, less lusty, more deliberate in nature. Their father, Yaná-uluha, being wise, readily saw the ways of the Sun Father and partaking of the Sun's breath, Yaná-uluha became among men as the Sun Father is to the little moons of the sky. He became Speaker to the Sun Father, keeper and giver of precious things and commandments, the first Sun Priest. He and his sisters became the seed of all priests of the midmost clan, the Master of the House of Houses.

The Winter and Summer People

Separation of the Clans

7
The Origin of Clans and Societies

Gathering the first Priest Fathers in council, the Beloved Twins met with them to select and name groups of men and the kinds of creatures and things. They decided that the Summer People belonged to the south where it was warm, and to the producing Earth Mother. The Winter People were made the children of the north and the quickening Sky Father.

In each of these groups there were people who liked one thing or another and understood it better than all others so that was selected for their name. Among the Summer People those who loved the sun became the Sun People, others who loved the water became the Frog, Turtle, or Toad clans. Still others who knew seeds became the First-Growing Grass or Tobacco People. Because the Badger liked the warm southern slopes and lived among the dry roots used for fire he and the ones who understood him became a part of the Summer People rather than being with the North People and the other animals. The Winter People according to their natures, talents, and inclinations became the Bear, the Coyote, and the Deer People. Others became the Turkey, the Crane, or the Grouse clans.

In this way the people were divided into clans, brothers and sisters who may not marry and who will cherish each other's offspring as their own. From each of these clans a headman was selected for instruction by the gods and the Father of the House of Houses, and was breathed upon by them. In this way these men became Masters of Secrets and the Keepers of Sacred Things. The Badger people were given the great shell whose core has an affinity for fire just as the Earth Mother is sensitive to earthquakes. Thus the younger and the elder Badger clan heads became the Keepers of the Shell and Wardens of Fire. The Winter People were given seed-substances for hail, snow, and new soil, the Water Peoples were given the seed of water, and to the still others, the germ of corn or tobacco was given.

When the foremost priests of more than one clan possessed the same kind of seed-substance or germ, they banded together to form a society for the better use and keeping of their medicines and various secrets, and for the guidance and care of their especial children. In this manner the leaders of the Bear, Crane, and Grouse clans became the Bearers of the Ice Wands. It is their prayers and powers that bring winter but at the same time ward off the accompanying evils of cold and illness.

In the beginning there were only four societies: the Shíwanakwe or priesthood of the Priest People; the Sániakiakwe, the priesthood of the Hunters who were from the Coyote, Eagle, and Deer clans and were keepers of the germ of game; the Áchiakiakwe, or Great Knife People who were the makers and defenders of pathways for the people; and the Néwekwe, keepers of magic medicines and knowledge, who were invincible against evil.

The Origin of Clans and Societies

Hardening of the Earth

8
The Hardening of the World

A s it was with creatures and men so it was with the world, for it was young and unstable. Its surface was dank like a marsh and seeds that were dropped upon it anywhere grew. Earthquakes shook the ground and strange monsters and demons of the deep Underworld came forth. Some of these creatures became fierce and preyed upon those that were timid; there was wretchedness and hunger; war and fear were everywhere. The frightened people became wanderers, hugging their scant possessions and living on the seeds of grasses and the dead and slain things. Ever eastward they were led by the Twins who told them that they must seek the light under the pathway of the Sun and find there the middle of the world where all would be stable and they could rest in peace.

For a while the trembling of the earth stilled and the people gathered at K'éyatiwanki, the Raised Place, yet they were still poor and defenseless. Each time the ground quaked, great demons and monsters fled forth to menace both men and creatures. At last the Twins took counsel with each other and the Sun Father and decided to bake the earth, to harden it by striking the ground with their lightning and thunder arrows. To protect the people from the devastation the Twins would shelter them with their cloud shields.

Standing one on one side of the people and the other opposite, the Two hurled their thunderbolts at the land. The din was dreadful as the mountains reeled and the heights split. Valleys cracked open and fires raged. The people who were shielded became soot-blackened and so filled with panic that they fell unconscious. At long last a heavy rain fell, quenching the fires and washing the face of the world. It cut deep trails downward in the surface and scattered the corpses of dead things or buried them deeply in the rocks and silt. Today streams of cool water run in the canyons cut by these fierce rains.

In other places the monsters, both great and small, clustered together and were there blasted. Their blood gushed forth and flowed deeply in streams and blackened into the dark rocks we see today. There were great dusty plains of bleached and stained soil streaked and banded from the heat of the Twins' lightning arrows. At last the heavings of the underground subsided and the earth, worn by the breath of ages, became divided one country from another.

Sheltered beneath the cloud shields of the Beloved Twins, the people survived and at last wakened, fearful, as from some dread dream, and began again to wander about the earth now solid and transformed beneath their feet. Led by the Beloved Two, the multitudes of people journeyed ever eastward pausing first at Tésak'ya Yala, the Place of Bare Mountains. Along the way they met others who had gone before and as fierceness had entered their hearts along with fear, they learned much in the ways of war. When at last they stopped at Támelan K'yaíyawan, Where the Trees Stand in Water, they had grown strong through fighting and many were headstrong, believing that they could stand alone.

And They Took Counsel

9
The Meeting of the Seed Peoples

They had not dwelt long at this place when the conch shells once again sounded and most of the people gathered their belongings to journey onward, leaving a few stubborn ones to perish miserably and alone. Passing through the land, they saw the smoke of many hearths and houses scattered about the hills before them. Coming closer they met those who lived in the houses at Shípololon K'yaía, or Steam Mist Rising from the Waters, and rudely challenged them. For they knew only warfare with strangers and hence demanded to know who they were and why they lived there.

The strangers replied, "We are the People of the Seed, born your elder brothers and led by the Gods!"

Whereupon our fathers, dark of understanding, grew more angry. "Not so," they said, "for truly, we are led by the gods and *we* are the Seed People for our elders carry the potent substance of seeds!"

The people who called themselves "of the Seed"—and were none other than the "Drinkers of the Dew of Grasses"—bade them pause. "Hold!"

33

they said, "We are wiser than you. We have powers beyond yours yet we cannot exert them without your aid, just as mothers may be fertile yet childless without fathers. You are our younger brothers. Your People of the Seed are more precious than they know, or you unwittingly boast of, for your people and their sacred keepings are like virgins, fertile but unrealized. Let us look peacefully upon one another. You therefore try your powers first, using the sacred things you carry in the manner in which you have devised or been instructed. We will then, according to our knowledge and practices, try our powers, thereby showing our customs to you."

At last after much wrangling and meeting in council, our fathers agreed to this and set eight days as the time to make their preparations for the contest. This was good for it won over the village people by wise and peaceful acts rather than by impetuous acts of violence.

Our fathers camped on the borders of the plain in the midst of the junipers and in the shade of the great pinyons. At the foot of the pinyons facing east they built a large bower of juniper, like the farm shelters of today. From this, our fathers and mothers, the priests and priest matrons of old, watched and labored, as young parents wait for the birth of their children, not knowing what appearance the offspring may have but expectantly glad of heart.

The Meeting of the Seed Peoples

There was a Sign in the Sky

10
The First-Growing-Grass Clan

Then the seed-priests, the master keepers of possessions, and those from the House of Houses, gathered and fasted, contemplating their sacred objects to divine their meanings. It seemed important to them to cut wands from the growth in open spaces, to paint them significantly, and add the plumes of the sun-loving summer and cloud birds. For they believed that through their incantations they could waft the breath of their prayers and their meanings to the far-sitting places of the ancients who had first taught them.

Before them the plain was dry and barren, needing fresh soil brought by torrents of hail as well as the nourishing moisture of rain for the germination of their seeds, so they might better demonstrate their powers to the strangers.

When all else was prepared they made a shrine and set within it their medicine seed of hail and soil (mú'etone), the seed of water and rain (k'yáetone), and their sacred seeds of grains (chúetone). Around these and reaching outward toward the Sun they placed plumed prayer wands. How-

37

ever, certain sage priests, to insure that their message might be clear and sure of favor, sought out the largest and most beautifully colored grass seeds and placed them in the gourd with their seed substances. They cut wood from the easily-growing, water-loving cottonwood and willow, added plumes and painted upon it each kind and color of the seed which they had selected.

When night came and the others slept, the master priests of the Seed Clan, from the First-Growing-Grass People, took their chúetone secretly to the plain in front of the bower where they breathed their prayers into these things and intoned the incantations taught them when the world was new. As the light of the seven great stars rose above they set the gourd upon the ground and placed wands about it. To the north they placed the first and brightest, the yellow grass seeds, then to the west the blue seeds, red ones went to the south and white to the east. The other three could not be planted where they should be—above the gourd, within it, and below it. As they sat thinking about this they saw among the stars that four were placed as though set about a gourd while three others led into it like a handle. Thinking it a sign from the Sun Father they set their black wand closest to the gourd, next the speckled one, and farthest out, the all-colored one pointing the way.

In the morning the watchers saw the plumes standing beautifully in the plain and asked who had planted them and for what. The priests replied, "They were planted in the night while you slept, by the seven stars." Misunderstanding, the people were overjoyed and said, "Seed wands of the stars themselves!" and delighted in the omen. During the eight days and nights, thick mists arose and the rain descended in torrents washing new soil evenly across the plain. On the ninth day as the clouds rolled away our fathers shouted happily to the other people against whom they were pitted, "Behold! Water and new soil, new grass, tall and plumed as were our wands, and spiked with seed, we bring where before there was only barren hardness. "Truly," cried the priests of the First-Growing-Grass People, the Aik'yaho-kwe, "*We* are the People of the Seed!"

The Origin of Corn

11
The People of the Dew

The People of the Dew heeded not the boasts of the First-Growing-Grass People. They acknowledged that new soil, water, and grasses had been brought forth but pointed out that no new life of either man or seeds had been produced. "Instead," they said, "come, let us work together to perfect what you have begun. We had none of what you possess, yet of the seed of seeds we are truly the people and our maidens are the mothers thereof, as you shall see."

They too set apart eight days for preparations saying, "That we may be perfect in the generation of the seed of seeds and in its abundance, send us forth from your numbers a youth of the Water clan, from those who possess the precious k'yáetone, and give this to us also, that we may join it to the chúetone you have placed in the midst of the growing plants according to our understanding of its meaning. And let the youth be handsome, perfect, and whole of seed."

Therefore the fathers of the people chose Yápot-uluha of the Water clan, foster child of the great Sunpriest Yaná-uluha. In his hand they placed the k'yáetone and certain prayer wands and sent him to the strangers, glorious to look upon.

Now in the village of the People of the Dew there were seven maidens, sisters of one house. Virgin foster children of Paíyatuma, the God of Dew, they were surpassingly beautiful and likened to the seven bright stars. Stories were told of them and songs were sung of them by their people. They too were chosen and breathed upon by the fathers and mothers of the People of the Dew and, with the youth Yápot-uluha, were instructed in the forthcoming rites.

All during the days of preparation a warm gentle rain fell. On the eighth day, the fathers and mothers led the maidens and the young man, all beautifully arrayed, down into the plain where the grasses grew before the bower from which the people watched. And there they danced and breathed from the sacred medicine seeds. All through the night they danced to the song of the elders, back and forth beside the plants, motioning the grasses upward with their prayer plumes, as we encourage the growth of plants today. As time went on the matron of the dance led the youth and the first maiden apart and had them grasp, one on either side, the first plant, and dance around it, gently drawing it up even as the Beloved Twins had caused the canes in the Underworld to grow. In like manner, the youth danced with each of the other maidens until all the plants had grown as tall as themselves, with joints showing where they had been grasped, and leaves like the plumage of the macaw.

In the night the Badger clan, keepers of the great shells, brought forth fire from the roots with their hands and placed it in the east so that its heat might take the place of the sun and its light give the dancers' acts more life. As dawn drew nigh, the mother-making matron approached and led the youth and the first maiden aside. Together they embraced the first of the full-grown plants, and so in turn did the youth and the other maidens embrace each of the remaining plants.

As they clasped the first plant, the fire in the east flamed brightly yellow with the first catching of the wood; as the couple clasped the second plant the flames were burning smokily with the fuller catching of the wood and the light was blue; as they encircled the third plant the fire reached mastery of the wood and its light was red. As they clasped the fourth plant the fire was fumeless and white its light; with the fifth plant the fire gave up its breath in a cloud of sparks. As they held the sixth plant the fire died down and its light was somber. Yet as they embraced the seventh plant, the fire wakened afresh in the winds of morning and glowed with a light of all colors.

Now as the day dawned, where the bodies of the youth and maidens had touched the plants, new parts appeared to the beholders. Showing through their coverings were many colors of seeds with soft hair shrouding them as if to make their beauty more precious.

The Visit of the Three

12
The Blessing of the Deities

As the people gazed in wonder at these marvelous plants with their many-colored seeds, three gods rose from the drifting mists in the east. First came forth the flute-playing child of the Sun, Paíyatuma, God of Dew and Music, followed by Ténatsali of the All-Colored Flowers, the God of Time and Directions, and then torchbearing Kwélele, God of Flame. Passing through the plants, Paíyatuma strengthened them with the invigorating breath of his flute. Ténatsali touched the plants with the essence of his flesh-renewing flowers while Kwélele hardened the seeds with the ripening flame of his torch. Then, as Paíyatuma waved his flute, Ténatsali, the seven Corn Maidens, and the attendant Kwélele, vanished into the mists of morning.

Lithe and tall, Paíyatuma turned to where the seven plants stood in the rising light of dawn and, standing forth like a traveler from afar before the amazed watchers, he said, "You children of men and the Earth Mother, Brothers of the Seed, Elder and Younger. Behold! The seed plant of all seeds! The grass seeds you planted were seen in the distant reaches of the stars and these regions are shown in their tassels. The plumes you planted were felt in far away spaces and are reflected in the shapes of their leaves. But the maidens are bright stars in the house of my children. Look well and cherish their persons nor change the gift of their being, for they shall be as fertile of flesh for all mankind as they would if bearing children for men. Lest you lose them, to seek in vain, be brothers. People, be Priests of the Corn for the seed of all seed plants is born.''

And as the people eagerly watched, the clouds of morning cleared away and gone with them, even as his words faded, was Paíyatuma, God of Dawn.

"We give thanks this day," together said our fathers and all the people as they looked upon the plants before them and at the strangers. "Truly, you are our older brothers and we will cherish your maidens and the fruit of their flesh even as our very own mothers cherish us."

"Yes," replied the other Seed People. "Eating thereof you will become in truth our younger brothers. For even as the Father has said, these are the products of our hands joined with yours in sacred thought."

Happily were our fathers joined to the People of the Dew. Thus many houses were built together near the plains where the corn plants first grew abundantly and where they were faithfully tended by the labors of the people and the vigils of their fathers.

Ka'wimosa's Children

13
The Search for the Middle

Time passed and the people had almost forgotten their search for the Middle when once again the shells sounded in warning. Gathering their children and their precious seed corn they journeyed on as one people, building great stone houses to live in on the hills, with shelters made of juniper branches in the valleys to watch over their sacred cornfields. But they wearied of the constant traveling and fell to devising ways that they might more effectively search for the Middle. They decided that by sending only a few in different directions to discover the great surrounding waters, they would soon locate the Middle without all having to move.

Now there was a priest named Ka'wimosa, Kachina Maker, so named because he unwittingly brought about the appearance of the kachinas among the Áshiwi, as our forefathers were called. This man had a daughter and four sons, the eldest of whom was called Kiaklo, for he was wise with words and understood all sounds. Thus when it was asked who should travel northward to learn the distance to the great encircling waters, Ka'wimosa thought of his eldest son. Kiaklo was summoned and duly

49

instructed in his duty while the priests planted prayer sticks to all of the deities for his safe journey and return. Then he departed.

But long the people waited and at last it was said, "Lost is our Kiaklo! Wise of words he was but not of ways."

Again the priests met and Ka'wimosa brought forth the two younger brothers of Kiaklo saying, "They will guide one another if you send two." After offering the appropriate prayers and instructions, the two, the Ána-hoho áchi, were sent southward with great hopes, but again no one returned.

Once more the council met and Ka'wimosa said, "Here!" and brought forth his youngest son and daughter. The boy, Síweluhsiwa, was a long-haired youth of great beauty matched only by that of his sister Síwiluhsitsa. Together they were brought forward and everyone made them ready. Then the two were sent eastward toward the rising sun.

Brother and sister journeyed far until before them rose a high mountain. When at last they reached it Síweluhsiwa built a juniper shelter for his sister to rest in while he went in search of food. When he returned with his game, his sister was asleep and as he sat beside her the wind moved her cotton mantle aside. Gazing at her, Síweluhsiwa became aroused and heedless of the consequences, he possessed her.

Now in those days the world was yet new and, like the supernatural beings, the forms of people were still changeable. Therefore, when Sí-wiluhsitsa pushed her brother from her in fright and shame and began to upbraid him in the harshest terms, she began to change. As she called him the most thoughtless and shameful of men, her eyes grew large and glaring and her face became mottled and drawn with emotion and slowly her hair turned white. In mortification Síweluhsiwa stood, at times dazed with his head bowed and his eyes red and swollen from weeping, and other times rushing about beating his head with his hands until great knobs and welts arose. Wet with sweat and tears, he threw himself to the ground rolling about until the red dust that clung to him hardened forever.

Síwiluhsitsa cried, "Know that neither you nor I may ever return to our people! We must forever live apart! By my power I will divide this mountain and you will live to the north and I will abide on the south." So saying she stamped her foot and deep was the mark she made, then drawing her sandal through the sands she scored the ground. The furrow deepened as the earth shuddered, as it did in those days, and the mountain divided in two and water welled up to flow ever faster and deeper as the two fled

The Search for the Middle

into the depths of the mountains. Some say they went together and others say apart, but in time strange children were born to these unnatural parents.

The first child, born of incestuous love before her parents changed, was womanly in shape yet of surpassing stature and strength—man and woman combined in one person. Not so with her nine brothers; they were male in appearance only but child-like, for sex was not in them. For as corn sown out of season does not ripen so the offspring of incest come to naught. These children were like their father and were as varied as his moods. Strapping dun-colored louts, marked with the weals and welts and distorted face of their father, they behaved one moment as simpletons speaking idiocies and yet uttering wise words and prophecies from the ancients the next. Nor were their names those of ordinary men but rather names expressing characteristics opposite of those they possessed. Thus the one named Pekwin, or Speaker of the Sun, had nothing to say while the one bearing the name of the Brave Bow Priest was an ardent coward, frightened of everything and everyone and unable to see real danger when it threatened. The Bat was afraid of shadows and unable to see in the dark, the Glum and Grumpy One, so named, was cheerful and helpful, the Ancient behaved as a youth while the Lad acted senile. Another hid ostrich-like behind a grass stem or a feather while his father, hands dangling, entranced by the inconsequential and giggling at the inappropriate, would in the next moment become the oracle of the ancients. Together, father and sons, they became the Koyemshi, the attendants and interpreters of the kachinas, as their name implies.

Search for the Middle

14
The Separation of the Clans

There came a time when the people who tarried could no longer await the return of the children of Ka'wimosa. Hearing the earth rumble, they readied for yet another journey. But the people had grown so vast in number that they could no longer travel together. Instead they were forced to divide, like herds of bison too numerous for the grass of a single plain.

The Bear, Crane, and Grouse clans of the Winter People, led by the Bearers of the Ice-Staffs and their precious mú'etone and the Brotherhood of the Knife, moved through the northernmost valleys.

Through the midmost valleys the Fathers of the People, the Keepers of the Seed, the Macaw clan and other Summer People were led by the Brotherhood of Priests, carrying with them their sacred k'yáetone.

The Keepers of Fire and the Seed Fathers of the Seed kin, carrying in their midst the precious chúetone, were guided by the Brotherhood of Paíyatuma, the Néwekwe, along with the Badger, Sun, and All-Seeds clans of the Summer People through the valleys to the south.

Far in front, first here and then there, the Beloved Twins scouted the way onward for the three groups. Like streams of water that flow apart and then rejoin, the people came together in seasons of rest before moving forward once more. As they moved forward in this order, they came in sight of the divided mountain of the Koyemshi.

Seeing the smoke and mist rising and believing that they were coming upon habitations of people, they all hurried forward. The Bear clan, always the most adventurous, was the first to approach and great was their dismay when, upon descending to the plain, they found a broad river flowing, not from east to west as had all the other rivers in their path, but northward. Lying directly across their path, the wide waters rolled sullen and turbid with the red soil from the plains to the south.

The Separation of the Clans

The Abode of Souls

15
The Abode of Souls

Not long did the impetuous Bear and Crane clan fathers deliberate, but straightway strode into the red waters feeling with their feet for footing as they led the way across. Yet their fearfulness was great for as they watched, the waters moved beneath them, strange chills and feelings beset them as though they were beginning to change into the forms of hidden water creatures. Nevertheless they won their way to the opposite shore. The poor women with children on their backs were more susceptible to the aura of these strange waters and became panic stricken and witless with fear. The children, being as yet unfinished and immature, changed instantly in their terror. Their skins turned cold and scaly and they grew tails. Their hands and feet became webbed and clawed as if for swimming in those disquieting waters. To their mothers the children felt like dead things that scratched and clung on their bare shoulders. Shrieking wildly, the mothers cast their children away and fled in terror.

Wailing piteously, many of the children fell into the swift waters. Their shrill and plaintive calls could be heard even from under the water—as it is said they may still be heard at night near lonely waters.

No sooner did they sink beneath the waters than they changed even more. Some became lizards, others frogs, turtles or newts. But their souls, their inner beings, sank through the waters of the lagoon below the hollow mountain of the Koyemshi into the abode of ghosts, Hápanawan, where the finished souls of ancient men of war and violent death resided. There also was the pueblo of Kóthluwalawan, the town of towns, with its great six-chambered assembly house of the spirits, wherein the god priests sat in council. It was there also that the priests taught to the newly dead the Kókokshi, or Dance of Good, and from them also received the messages and offerings of mortal men.

Now when the little ones sank into the dark depths, the lights of the spirit dancers began to break upon them and they became as the ancients. Having been received by these undying ones, they thus made the pathway that all the dead must follow. But the mothers, not knowing their children had returned unharmed to the spirit world where in time they too would go, loudly wailed on the far shore of the river.

The Seed clans were the next to arrive and they also strove to cross the waters only to meet the same dismal fate. Upon witnessing this, the Macaw and the other midmost clans fled southward looking for a better crossing and were soon lost from view never to be seen again.

As the people wailed and mourned their lost children, the Beloved Twins returned and with strong sounding voices bade them cease their clamor and terror. They advised all mothers to cherish their children through all dangers and not behave like birds, abandoning their offspring at the first threat. "For," they said, "the magic of the waters will pass when you leave them and all will be as before!" Thus those who had yet to pass through the river took heart and clutching their children to them they won their way through the waters to the opposite shore.

Now when the people were rested and the remaining children calmed, they arose and journeyed into the plain east of the two mountains with the great water between. Thence they turned northward to camp on the sunrise slopes of the uppermost mountains. Mourning their lost children, they also awaited the ones who had fled southward, but those never returned.

Kiaklo Goes Home

16
The Journeys of Kiaklo

Throughout this time the all-hearing and wise-of-speech Kiaklo had been journeying alone into a north land of cold white desolation, lost in a world hidden beneath the snow that lies forever there. His face had become wan and covered with the frozen mists of his breath until it was as white as the creatures who lived in that dread land. So cold and dreary of heart, blinded by the light, he wept constantly and the tears that streamed down his face forever stained it. His lips cracked from calling out continuously and his voice grew shrill and dry-sounding like the voices of the far-flying waterfowl, until at last his heart within him died and he became transformed and everlasting as are the gods. As he cried, wandering blindly hither and thither, the water birds flocked about him cocking their heads and calling to one another. But even though he heard and understood their speech, he lamented anew for none told him the way to his country and people.

Now when the Duck heard his cry, it sounded like her own so she drew close answering loudly. When they came together, they seemed to be strangely kin. As he was the listener and speaker, the wisest of all men, she was from every region and familiar with all ways and directions even above and below water, and so the most knowing of all creatures. Thus the wisdom of the one understood the knowledge of the other.

Kiaklo besought the counsel and guidance of the duck, crying "Oh Grandmother! Where am I, strayed so far from my country and people? In councils of men I know all, but of the far ways I know naught. The mountains, valleys, and plains are white and even the light of the sun makes all ways more hidden in whiteness. In the brightness my eyes see only darkness and all ways are bewildering. The wind speaks to me of all regions but not of the direction to the Middle or to my people!"

"Hold, my father!" said the Duck, "Think sad thoughts no longer, for though you are blind yet you hear all, as I see all. Give me the tinkling shells from your belt, place them about my neck and follow their sound, and I will lead you to your people whom I know well."

Kiaklo took the talking shells he had always worn from his belt and placed them on the neck and in the beak of the Duck, then lamely and painfully followed the sound of the bells. As she flew before him from place to place, she paused to duck her head and dip her beak so the shells would sound more loudly. At last they came to the country of heavy rains and thick mists on the borders of the snow world. They passed from water to water until finally a wider expanse of water lay before them. In vain the Duck jingled the shells but Kiaklo, who could neither swim nor fly, was unable to follow her.

Now the Rainbow Worm was nearby for his home was in the land of mists. Hearing the sound of the shells he thought, "Ha! These are my grandchildren for they call one another with the shells of the encircling waters!" So in one measure of his length he placed himself nearby, saying, "Why do you cry out? Give me plumes that I may be uplifted to cloud heights. My footsteps will be from country to country and I will bear you upon my shoulders to your people and their country."

Kiaklo took from his pouch the lightest and choicest prayer plumes and, with two strong pinion feathers that Duck gave to make his prayers far-reaching, tied them together. Rainbow arched himself and stooped down nearby. Then Kiaklo breathed on the plumes and approaching, fastened them to Rainbow's near side. With bent head, all white and glistening, Kiaklo said the sacred words, looking neither to the right nor the left, and as he did so the shadow of Rainbow gleamed brightly on his forehead like a tiny rainbow and remained there everlastingly painted.

Rainbow said, "Thanks this day! Now mount on my shoulders." Then he arched himself high amidst the clouds, bearing Kiaḱlo upward as a particle of dust is wafted on the breeze. Duck spread her wings in flight to the south and Rainbow Worm straightened himself and like an arrow followed until they reached the Lake of the Ancients whose mists were as the breath of life to him. In that plain north of Kóthluwalanne, Rainbow set Kiaḱlo down and returned to the land of mists. Kiaḱlo, weary and lame, sat down to rest and ponder.

Now as he sat there, the child-like clamor and harangues of the Koyemshi loudly calling to one another reached his ears, and he learned of the people who had crossed the river with so much trouble and commotion and who had gone on eastward. The shame of the parents of the Koyemshi was so great they only wanted to hide. Hence they told their offspring nothing of their kinship to the grieving Áshiwi. But Kiaḱlo, who heard and understood all, knew from the Koyemshi's talk who they were, what had befallen his own brother and sister and all the evils brought to his people by the sin and change-making of these two. With this comprehension, the strength of his heart wasted away and he bowed down on the plain, alone, blinded of sight, weary and lame, rendered senseless by the woes of his brother and sister and what their action had wrought. In vain the Duck shook her shells ever again as Kiaḱlo sat bereft of all thought, lamenting his brother and sister's deed and the travails of his people.

The Journey of Kiaklo

17
Kiaklo and the Council of the Gods

In desperation the Duck flew toward the mountain from whence all the garrulous talking of the Koyemshi came, but as she went she spied the lake in its hollow below and settled there. Back and forth, she swam up and down, quacking in distress and calling out, when Lo! the lights of the kíwitsin, the kiva of the gods, began to gleam in the lake. As Duck gazed, there came the Sálimopia of the North rising beak first like one of her own kind, dispatched to bring her and her message to the great council hall. Diving down she followed the Sálimopia into the presence of Páutiwa, Chief of Kóthluwalawan, and all the other gods, where she told of Kiaklo sitting blind, lame, and bereft of his senses, in the plain north of the mountains.

"Well we know him!" said the gods. "His mother and father breathed of our sacred breath when the world was new and when their time is finished, they will join us here. Because Kiaklo was changed violently by his grief and sore hardships while yet unfinished, he has been transformed and will remain forever as he is. He will continue, without end, as one of

65

us. This is also true of his brother and sister and their uncouth offspring in the nearby mountain. Therefore, go to the lake shore and entice these offspring to its bank with your shells. Loudly they will clamor and marvel but they will give the old ones no peace until they come. When they see the necklace of shells they will instantly become grave and listen to your words. Bid them, but not their sister, to make a litter of poles and reeds and bear Kiaklo hither. They may not enter here but can point the way to our presence for him who has become as one of us. They also are of us, save that they have placed themselves between the living and the dead by their own rash act and must for all time point the way of those who live again, the newly dead. Tell Kiaklo not to tarry but to come straight away and learn of his ancestors and the past and how events shall be in the future."

The Duck did as she was bidden and even as the gods had said, the Koyemshi boisterously made a litter and, singing happily, they went to where Kiaklo sat dazed in misery. When Kiaklo looked upon them in the starlight he wept. So too wept the Koyemshi's father, he who had been the glorious Síweluhsiwa, even as he sang his soothing dirge. Then suddenly gleeful as a child, he capered about cajoling Kiaklo into getting on the litter. Shouting and gamboling, the Koyemshi carried him away to the great black lake wherein gleamed the lights of the dead.

From the depths rose the Sálimopia of All Directions and taking Kiaklo on their shoulders, they bore him out over the lake to a ladder of rushes and canes that rose by itself high out of the water. Kiaklo, scattering prayer meal before him, stepped upon it with the slow movements of a blind man entering a roof hole. No sooner had he taken four steps than the ladder sank into the depths and the lights winked out. But when the Sálimopia entered the darkened great council hall with Kiaklo, the Little Fire God, Shúlawitsi, lifted his torch on high, and swinging it about, lighted all the fires anew so that the lights shone and Kiaklo saw again with the fullness of his sight. Revealed to him were all of the assembled gods and soul-beings as each Sálimopia took his place at the entry to one of the six chambers leading from the hall.

Páutiwa then welcomed Kiaklo saying, "Sit down with us that we may speak, for you have wandered afar and become changed. As a woman is loved because she maintains her family line, so shall you, tireless listener to all sounds of meaning, be cherished among us and sacred to mortal men. You shall keep unbroken for men the story of Creation which we shall relate, and of all the past and future.''

Listening, Kiaḱlo sat down and extended his hand. And Duck who had guided him, came and stood upon it as though resting on a wave or branch.

The gods then sent their messengers, the swift Sálimopia and the fleet but timid Héhea, to summon all beings to gather in the sacred dance circle of the Kókokshi. And with those who came were the Little Ones who had sunk beneath the waters, now well and beautiful, clad in cotton mantles and necklaces, sad only because their mothers still lived above. When the dance was completed the gods said, ''Let us begin.''

Kiaḱlo answered, saying: ''It is well. I am ready, even my heart listens!'' Then each god told Kiaḱlo the things he best knew as Kiaḱlo kept time to the cadence, moving the Duck with her tinkling talking shells as a master of song moves his baton or a dancer his rattle. This same message he speaks today when he comes among us for the welfare of our children, bringing the life breath of the kachinas for boy and man alike.

When after a long time they had finished, the gods further charged him with a comforting message for the mothers of the lost Little Ones and with instructions for men and beings. After the sacred cigarette was brought, the gods and Kiaḱlo smoked to the six directions and then the gods placed Kiaḱlo's hand upon the door of each of the chambers so he might know the place of worship even in the dark though it was night or he was dim of vision. They charged him with relating the customs and words of the gods to all of those who hold the rites of the kachinas.

The Sálimopia then lifted the ladder and guided Kiaḱlo and the Duck to the shore of the lake. Drawn by the tinkling of the shells, the Koyemshi came, playing and singing and carrying their litter, for much they loved Kiaḱlo in the light of the day, as a raven loves bright shells or chips of stone.

How Kiaklo came to his People.

18
How Kiaklo Came to His People

The Koyemshi sobered instantly and assumed a grave mien as they neared Kiaklo, who bade them listen to the words and instructions of the gods as related to him. "You shall be the guardians of the kachinas, the ones who speak their meanings, and shall give great enjoyment to the children of men even as you did for me in my sorrow on the plain. You will take me to the people yonder, for I have tidings for them and instructions which you must witness for the times when I am not about. You will cherish the kachinas and all other customs because like your father, my younger brother, and your elder sister, the man-woman of the kachinas, you have become fitted for all time to their ways, even as I have become slave yet master at their councils. But my sister, your mother, shall abide always in the place she has made as women always maintain the hearths of men.

Upon completing this speech, Kiaklo seated himself upon the litter and the Koyemshi obediently bore him eastward along the path the dead follow back to the westward when they have reached their fulfillment.

Calling back and forth to one another in happy clamor as they went, the Koyemshi so amused the People of the Prairie Dog Villages that all of them came out to watch them go by. The Koyemshi in turn were so pleased with this audience that they began to sing. Their gleeful noise as they approached the Áshiwi camp disarmed the fears of the people who gathered to wonder at the strange procession of capering, singing beings, bearing someone on a litter and led by a duck. Just so do we still happily and expectantly await their coming and our young wonder as did the first men of that day.

Prompted by the Twins who led them, the elders belatedly recognized Kiaklo as their long lost traveler and treated him with the respect accorded a returning relative. Lest evil enter also, they carefully housed him apart and smoked a purifying cigarette before receiving Kiaklo in secret council. Treating him as one who is famished, they sparingly fed Kiaklo only a corn flour drink, but upon his companions, the Koyemshi, they heaped gifts of food and clothing.

Kiaklo then presented his message of comfort about the little children lost in the waters and how mothers and fathers would see them again when they had fulfilled their time and traveled westward along the path of the dead to Kóthluwalawan. Taking the Duck, his guide in blindness, onto his hand, Kiaklo spoke in solemn, measured tones. Keeping the cadence of the deities' words with the sound of the shells about the Duck's neck, he related the words of creation, the tale of his wanderings, the speeches of the gods, and the sacred customs required for each direction. In each of the six councils he presented these words so no part would be forgotten. Thus did our forefathers learn of those who went searching and of the fate of the little children lost in the river. They also learned of how the spirit beings, those dead before time, man and animals, and even the lost clans, would gather with the passage of time in the spirit village of Kóthluwalawan.

When Kiaklo had finished speaking, he and the Koyemshi breathed into the nostrils of those who had listened to seal their relationship for all time. Whereupon the Koyemshi, amid laughter and loud jokes about their welcome, the gifts they received, and their desire to return, bore Kiaklo away upon his litter away to the mountain and the City of the Kachinas, Kóthluwalawan.

How Kiaklo Came to His People

Return of the Brothers Ánahoho

19
Return of the Brothers Ánahoho

S carcely had they departed when two strangers, seemingly guided by
Sálimopia and other swift runners of the kachinas, appeared from the
west. Feared by all the people then as they are now by the children, these
kachinas were fierce and whipped the people from their pathway to make
room for those they guided. For the two were none other than the brothers, Ánahoho, who had returned to find only the desolated villages of their
people. In vain had they sought for the living in the blackened and desert-
ed houses. Always seeking their brother Kiaklo, they even looked in storage
vessels and tore down chimneys to peer within as they searched. When
they did not find him, they smote their faces and held their noses in grief.
Their soot-blackened hands marked their faces which became flattened and
masked by the black handmarks of their dismay and they cried long and
dismally.

No sooner had Ánahoho entered the village, led by the kachinas, than
they began turning over the things left by the people in their fear. Rushing
over the rooftops, the two threw everything they found crashing to the

ground below. There the Sálimopia trampled these things into the earth so they might go the way of the dead. Seeing this, the people brought out all manner of vessels and baskets into which the Ánahoho peered, searching, then cast them down and gave their dreary mournful cry.

Thus to this day they follow their brother, never finding but always seeking, sending to their brother the souls of men's possessions that all may be well for them in the afterlife.

The Making of Men

20
The Great Journey Renewed

Long tarried the people in the town on the sunrise slope of Koyemshi Mountain, loath to leave the place of the kachinas and the lake with their dead children. Also they were awaiting the return of their lost clans. But the rumbling of the earth grew louder and at last they called the Twins, who bade the people, now fewer in number, to rise and join together and follow them eastward to seek the Middle. However, not long into their journey, they came upon a place of great promise where they decided to remain as perhaps it might be the Middle. Here they built larger and better structures than ever before and named their great stone building Hán'th- lipíngkia, the "Place of the Sacred Stealing." Even though they prospered here, they met now and again older nations of men, and struggled with them. But they gained little except greater danger to themselves in their increasing anger and stubbornness. Therefore the elders of all the clans convened and sought council with their gods.

"Changed you are and more changed shall you be!" said the Twins in such voice and fashion that none failed to heed. "Men you shall now be, walking straight in the pathways, clothed in garments, and tailless. Your feet shall be webless and your hands void of talons, yet fit for fighting!"

Then, in processions like dancers, the clans were ranged. First their forelocks were shorn by the Twain with their weapons of lightning that the Sun might know them as his children. Again they formed in procession as their webbed fingers were split and their webbed toes parted with knives of lightning. Sore were the wounded and the foolish cried aloud, but the gods made them bear all that they be made better men. Once more the procession was aligned and the tails of men were sharply razed. There were many who cried loudly, little heeding the first who no longer considered the pain they had suffered, and fled away in terror to the south where they may still be seen by far travelers, long of tail and hand, wizened man-children, wild and noisy, eating raw things like the creatures. Thus say the words of the ancients about those who greatly feared the words of their fathers yet failed to heed their warnings.

The Call to the Chiefs of Direction

21
The Twin War Gods and
the Origin of the Priests of the Bow

A nd there came a time when the people grew vain and waxed insolent
saying: "Surely we have attained the Middle or some place equal to
it. Let us build greatly and lay up stores and not wander again though the
earth trembles and the Two bid us to come forth. We will be strong and
defy all that is fearful!" But even as they spoke the distant mountains
trembled.

Well aware that the temper of the people had changed, the spirit of
the Beloved Twins changed also and they said, "Truly a time has come
and this is the time." Thereupon they called forth the elders of the Midmost clan and of all the folk clans and the men of the Great Knife to council and spoke thus: "Long have you dwelt here at rest from journeying.
You have become stronger, grown lusty and vain, and seek to live apart
from your fathers. You have changed! Changed while yet far from the
world's stable Middle. Yet you boast you have found it and think about
warfare! Proven you shall be! Thus far we have led you in peace and with
counsel and by wisdom controlled you. But we too have changed by

wounding our children with weapons of magic and tasting their blood. Henceforth by the power of war and with the hazards of omens and chance we shall open the way and guide the search for the Middle. Our names shall be known as the Áhaiyuta, the Twins Who Hold the High Places of Earth; the elder and foremost is Úyuyewi while Mátsailema is the younger of birth and the follower."

"Come forth, you War Men of the Knife, make wands of prayer feathers for death and spaces. Bring out the great drum of the regions. Come forth, master priest of the North, first kin of the Bear, bring out the seedstuff of hail and tempests! Come forth, master priest of the West, first kin of the Coyote, bring out the seedstuff of animal slaying! Come forth, master priest of the South, first kin of Badger, and bring out the shell trumpets of fire! Come forth, master priest of the East, first kin of the Turkey, bring out the great crystal of light! Come forth, master priest of the Zenith, first kin of the Eagle, lay before us the streaked stone of Lightning! Come forth, master priest of the Nadir, first kin of the Snake, lay out the black stone of Thunder! Sit apart you priests of the Middle, first kin of all People. Know well your seed-things and children! Speak wisely to these, our new children, for they shall be your first speakers and the peace-making shields of your people, even though they feed the soil with the blood of your foes!"

Then the Twins gave directions, setting aside eight days for preparations, each to his own. When all had been done as commanded they assembled around the deep pool in the valley that leads to walled Hán'thlipíngkia. Here the sacred seeds, hearts of the clans, were gathered, and in their midst was placed the great drum jar, all this encircled first by the clan elders and then by the priests and lastly by the knife-bearing warriors.

Softly the Twins chanted the sacred song measure—the magical and dread shomitakia—and whispered the seven deadly names! Then they painted the round mark of thunder and the wavering trail of lightning around the great drum. With prayer dust they marked the cross of the quarters over the drumhead just as they had marked the cloud shields when they had leveled firebolts to the four regions of the earth. With glittering black iron they painted the eyes of the leaders, and with their own blood they tinged the cheeks of the assembled warriors. The Twins sealed every lip with the pollen of sleep and into the nostrils of each they breathed to give power to men's voices in battle and to strengthen men's wills with endurance. Then they said to the drummer and singers: "Now you shall sing

Zuni Warrior

our dread song and you will perish like beetles falling in ashes! But in the lightning and windstorms your beings will join the Beloved Two and your breaths shall strengthen the warriors and give power to their voices. You shall be foremost, forever our chosen, the Priests of the Bow! The people shall see that we do not fear the coming of fireblasts and thunder for our name-fathers will be fiercer than any of the storm gods of the six directions.

But we Two shall be changed in being, made black and misshapen, made stronger with fierceness, swifter with hurling, more crafty in the turning. Plunged deep into the waters we shall emerge renewed in vigor that you may be led upward. So that men may be kept living, you Priests of the Bow shall multiply the means of destruction to be put into their hands. But our singers and drummer, grouped in song for our chosen, will be changed to age-enduring rock, the footrests for eagles and the sign of our order."

The elders bowed their heads in thought and secretly prayed in their hearts. The people who watched held their breaths and covered their mouths with their robes in fear of the powers of magic and with woe for their fathers.

To the right and the left of the water the Gods took stands, as they had stood by the cloud shield with their weapons between them. To the east the prayer feathers of the warriors were placed in lines. The warriors, ready for travel, circled about the lines but apart from them. Then turning the Two gave the word of beginning. The master of words raised his staff with its plumes of the men and the drum master lifted high his drum hoop, the symbol of thunder with the red of lightning on its handle. Six times they lifted in silence and then struck with the might of their sinews! The sound shook the valley with thunder that echoed above and reverberated below. The sacred meal on the drumhead lifted and danced like a rain cloud about them. The waters below moved and bubbled, mists like a cold breath ascended and, as wind in a vessel, the song sounded. Black cloud steps reared up from the four quarters of the world and darkened the day with their shadows.

When the first name was sung by the singers, the world rocked with thunder and earthquakes and the roar of swift storms coming from the northland. Ha'thl'tunkia, with staring eyes yellow as firelight in the winter and teeth gnashing in rage and stained as aged corn shucks, rumbled down

Saishiwani

from the north with his pelting hail, mingled with mud and deep water. In a voice like a torrent he bellowed loud to the Twins and singers: "Why do you call, you small worms of the waters, spawn of the earth and its quarters, shameless disturbers of thought. Why do you call my name?"

"Stay your feet in patience, Grandfather, we are small but we rejoice in your fury, yearn for your counsel and spirit, for we long to smite foes from the pathways as you cast trees from the highlands!"

"Being so, it is well," said the ancient, and the seedstuff of hail, bound with treasure, gleamed with ice from the breath of his answer.

When they sang the next name of the song, Úheponolo rolled in from the west land in sand blasts with dust clouds like mountains and stayed their feet with his drifting, but he also gave them what they desired. As Óloma's name was called, he swirled up from the southland like a fire draft and cracked the pool rim, yet he too gave them what they asked. With the fourth name, Tsaí'luh'tsanokia, shrieking shrilly, shot the mountains and valleys with dawn frost before complying with their request. Then they named Saushúlima who streamed down from his domain, the Zenith, and deluged the valley with swift water before this ancient also complied. As they called the sixth name, that of Saishíwani, the storm chief of the Nadir, the earth ripped open and ghosts, corpses and demons of blackness writhed forth in hot flames from the chasm and hurled the gods into the water! Black smoke rose and strangled the people who fell as though struck by lightning. It stiffened the drummer and singers whose song ceased as they weakly called forth the last name, Unahsinte, the storm chief of All Directions. Whirling in, twisting trees like a spinner twists yucca string, Unahsinte plucked the Twins from the hot surging waters and dried the foam in their hair into war bonnets. Seizing his brothers he hurled each back to his mountain or his position Above and Below. Then rising, he lifted the smoke clouds and there bending above, alight with sunshine, was the Rainbow.

The drummer and singers still sat, but were now changed forever by the power of the ancients. Partly covered by the dust swept around them, made stark by the roar of the death sounds, fixed in death by the shock of lightnings, burned hard by the frost-mingled fire drafts, they still remain, their drum in the middle, forevermore in that valley.

Now dwarfed and hideous were Úyuyewi and Mátsailema, formerly the Beloved Two Who Descended, and strong with the power of evil. They were armed as were the warriors of old with long bows and black stone-tipped cane arrows carried in long-tailed catamount-skin quivers; with slings and death-dealing stones carried in fiber pockets; spear throwers and blood-drinking broad knives of gray stone in fur pouches; short face-pulping war clubs thrust aslant in their girdles; and shields of cotton plaited with yucca upon their backs. About their bodies they wore casings of scorched rawhide, horn-like in hardness, while upon their heads were helmets like the neck-hide of the elks from which they came.

Small were the Two and misshapen, but strong and hard-favored, unyielding of will, heartless and wily, wrathful of heart and strong of spirit; they were evil. They were masters of chance and fate for they carried the arrows of destiny, like the regions of men, four in number. They carried the shuttlecocks of divination and the tubes of hidden things, four in number, as well as the revealing balls. They bore other things as well—the feather bow and plume arrow of far-finding, tipped with the shell of heart-searching, and the race sticks of swift journeys and way-winning—all of these things to divine men's chances and to play games of hazard, wagering the fate of whole nations in mere pastime.

Two children of terror and magic they were and when they called with the voice of destruction the downed warriors stirred and arose breathing battlecries. Swiftly they aroused those who still lived of the deep-slumbering people. Some, like the drummer and singers, had stiffened to stone. Years come and go but hunters see them still sitting or lying where they were stricken. Others survived and were led back to rebuild their devastated homes by the priests. Again the Twins assembled their warriors saying, "You are our chosen. Not long shall we tarry, therefore prepare for journeys with weapons and clothing like our own. Attend our teaching at night in hidden places for your strength shall lie in straight thinking where there is confusion all about." Then night after night the war drum sounded deep in the caves of the valley, potent and secret, as the War Gods taught the first Priests of the Bow. Thus were the Priests of the Bow established by the teachings of the Twin War Gods and none might gainsay, not even the fathers whose speakers they were, and none might contend, not even the sorcerers whose scourge they were.

Chákwaina Ókyatsiki

22
War With the Black People

One dark night the world groaned and again the shells sounded warnings. Together the Two War Gods, the Áhaiyuta, and their new warriors sought out the elders and bade them take their possessions in hand. Swiftly and sternly they awakened the sleepers, old and young, and those who obeyed were gathered in clan lines and marched away to safety. Úyuyewi and his warriors led the way, with Mátsailema and his warriors following, shields of the people, the makers and destroyers of pathways.

In time their journey eastward led them to plains in the midst of which were great heights with large towns built upon them. The fields were many and the possessions of these people were abundant for they knew how to command and carry the waters, bringing new soil, and this without either hail or rain. And so the ancients, the Áshiwi, hungry from long wandering, gave them battle.

Now these people of the highlands and cliffs were the Kianakwe of the elder nations of men and allied to the Ákakakwe, the People of Acoma. Before the four days of fighting were over, the Áshiwi were nearly defeated.

For it was here that Kúyapalitsa, the Chákwaina Ókyatsiki or Ancient Warrior Woman, led the enemy with shrill cries, shaking her rattle, and thus the fighting fell ill for our forefathers, the Áshiwi. Moreover the thunder boomed and confused the warriors and the rain fell, stretching their bow strings of sinew and quenching the flight of their arrows.

But on the second day the strong-hearted Thlétokwe or Wood Society devised bow strings of yucca fiber that did not stretch in the rain and brought forth the finest arrowheads made from the stones on the flanks of Koyemshi Mountain. Strengthened by the kachinas brought from Kóthluwalawan by the Two War Gods, they pressed forward once more. And again Kúyapalitsa, heedless of wounds to her body, ran back and forth in front of her army shrieking and shaking her rattle. The Kianakwe, emboldened by her actions, succeeded in capturing four of the gods of Áshiwi: Shalako, the courier of the rainmaking uwannami; Saíyathlia, one of the Warrior Gods; Ifsepasha, the game-making Koyemshi; and one of the beautiful kachinas, the Kókokshi. When both sides fell back on the evening of the third day, the Kianakwe held a victory celebration and paraded their captives before their people. But in the commotion Shalako escaped, fleeing so rapidly none could overtake him. It was then that the Two War Gods sought the counsel of their Sun Father about the deathless Warrior Woman and the knowledge came to them that her heart was carried in her rattle.

Shrouded in veils of falling rain, the warriors of both sides drew together on the fourth morning, whereupon the elder War God Úyuyewi aimed his arrow and, piercing her rattle, saw Kúyapalitsa fall dead. In panic her people fled the pursuing Áshiwi, who paused only to free the captives before entering the great town. Hidden deep in the cellars beneath the town, they found survivors blackened by their own war magic and plucked them out like rats from a hollow juniper. As these survivors were wiser and more comely than the common man, they spared them, and called them the Kwínikwakwe, the Black Corn People, and received them into the clan of the Black Corn.

Now for once the Warriors of the Bow were surfeited with fighting and paused to rest. Brothers, elder and younger, clasped the hands of the vanquished and in time held speech with them, for at first these people were wild of tongue. Thereby our fathers gained much knowledge, even of their own powers and possessions, from the Black People, in the same manner they had gained knowledge from the People of the Dew. Growing wiser in the ways of living, they learned to cherish their corn more, discovering they might have life and abundance rather than cause death and hunger. Yet still their journeyings were not ended.

Shípapolima

23

The Clans Divide in Their Search for The Middle

When once again the Two Little Ones, Úyuyewi and Mátsailema, bade the Áshiwi arise and seek the Middle, they divided them into great companies that they might fare better. Again the Winter People were bidden to go northward as their strength would enable them to overcome obstacles and their yucca-strung bows could win over their enemies no matter what the weather, rainy or dry. Led by Mátsailema and his Priests of the Bow they carried their precious mú'etone, the seedstuff of hail. Surrounded by the Warriors of the Knife and aided by the wily Thlétokwe, the Winter People fought their way northward. When they reached the valley of the Snow-Water River (Úk'yawane), the Rio Puerco of the West, they settled first at the mud-issuing springs of that valley and built Hékwainankwin, where the mounds of their villages may be seen to this day and the marks of their rites and their clan names are seen on the rocks thereabouts. Still they wandered on, building sometimes in the plains and again in the cliffs, until at last they reached Shípapolima, the Sacred City of the

Mists. Here in the land of the sacred Brotherhoods they learned of Pó-shaiyangkia, the Master Curer, before wandering farther on down the Rio Grande to the ancient village of Chipía. From there they turned westward to the mountains of Shíwina Yálawan, settling finally at Ta'iya, the Place of Planting.

Southward the People of Corn and Seeds moved, guided by the Kwínikwakwe. Following the valley of the river of Red Flowing Waters, they built large towns of great beauty as may be seen to this day, towns divided by clans yet joined as a whole. Far south they continued until they came into the great valley of Shókoniman, the home of the flute canes, beneath Shóko Yálanne, the Mountain of Flutes, where they turned eastward. Constantly contending with the Ka'ka People they fought their way to finally reach the Mountain of Space Markings, Yála Tétsinapa, before turning back westward to settle at last in Shíwina Téu'thlkwaina in the upper Zuni valley. Here they built their town of Héshotatsina and many others, all of them round and divided in parts, before they rejoined the People of the Middle.

The People of the Middle, the Macaw people and their children, led by Úyuyewi, his warriors, and the fathers of all the people, journeyed straight eastward to settle at Kwá'kina. It was here that Mákekwe, the Brotherhood of Fire, originated, bringing to its members the ability to pass unscathed through the flames. Here also arose the dance drama of the Mountain Sheep. After the ancient fathers built Kwá'kina the earth rumbled and the shells sounded, but not as loudly as before, so the people no longer rose as a body to seek the Middle. Some remained despite the dangers while others moved on. At each place, the people stopped and built greatly, becoming in time the fathers of "Those Who Dwell Around the Middle." It was in this way that first after Kwá'kina, Háwikuh was built. Then followed K'yánawe, Hámpasawan, Kyakime, and Mátsaki. Of those abiding, each group believed it had found the Middle, at least for itself, until towns lay in each of the directions. Still the People of the Macaw and other midmost clans sought patiently for the Middle until at last they thought they had found it in Mátsaki.

Secure in this belief, the Macaw People tarried there where they were found by the Peoples of Corn and Seed who had seen their smoke. These

The Clans Divide in Their Search for The Middle

people who were living in round houses to the eastward, were addressed by the Macaw, "You are our younger brothers! At Mátsaki here in the Middle let us dwell in peace as one people. Others of our kind are about us, yet with us." Thereby Mátsaki greatly increased, yet still the warnings sounded and gods and master-priests could not rest.

K'yanas' tipe, the Water Skate

24
The Great Council of Men and Beings

Worrying what portent these rumblings conveyed, the priest fathers called a great council of men and beings to determine once and for all the exact location of the Middle. After long deliberation they decided that if they could locate the outermost parts of the six regions they could more easily determine the Middle where they met. Then it was that someone said; "Where is K'yanas'tipe, the Water Skate? Six legs he has and of great length."

Thereupon being summoned, K'yanas'tipe appeared, growing ever larger, for it was the Sun-Father in the Water Skate's semblance. And he answered, "Very well, that I can do!" even before they had asked the question. Lifting himself to the heavens he extended his six finger-feet in all six directions so they touched the great waters to the north, west, south, and east, and they touched the waters above to the northeast, the waters below to the southwest.

But to the north his finger-foot grew cold so he drew it in; and to the west, the waters being nearer, he drew in his finger-foot also. But to the

97

south and east, he stretched his finger-feet far. Then gradually he settled downward and called out, "Where my heart and navel rest, beneath them mark the spot and build your town there for that shall be the midmost place of Mother Earth, albeit not the center because of the nearness of cold to the north and waters to the west. As he squatted over the middle of the plain and valley of Zuni, he drew in his legs and his feet marked the trails leading outward like the radiating web of a spider.

The fathers of the people built on this spot and rested their fetishes there, but unbeknownst to them K'yanas'tipe had swerved a little to the south in lowering his body. Nevertheless, the warnings no longer sounded and, because of their good fortune in finding the stable Middle of the World, the priest fathers called this midmost town Halónawan and built greatly.

The Great Council of Men and Beings

Ko'loowisi, the Plumed Water Serpent

25
Corn Mountain and the Great Flood

However the Áshiwi were not destined to remain undisturbed. Because they had erred ever so slightly evil again befell them. Rain came and the river rising, full swollen, ran to the southward and, breaking from its pathway, cut the great town in half, burying both people and houses in mud. Those who had not perished in the great town gathered together with neighbors from other flooded towns, and fled in desperation to the top of a nearby mesa, bearing with them all the corn they could find that had not been washed away. Because of the corn they carried to the mesa top they called it Corn Mountain (Dówa Yalánne).

But the water continued to rise and although Dówa Yálanne towered hundreds of feet above the flooded valley floor, the people feared for their lives. Rising steadily, the waters were nearing the summit when the great water serpent, Ko'loowisi, came swimming in from the west and rested his plumed head on the soaring flank of Dówa Yalánne, marking forever the rocks of the mountain with the imprint of his massive jaw.

It was then that the people in consternation feared the flood would sweep them from the summit if nothing was done. A council was called and it was at last decided that only a human sacrifice would stop the inexorable rise of the waters. Selecting the most perfect son and daughter of one of the Rain Priests, they dressed them in beautiful clothes and adorned them with necklaces of precious stones and shells. Hand in hand the boy and girl walked into the great sea and disappeared beneath the waters. No sooner had they disappeared than Ko'loowisi sank beneath the waters and the enveloping sea began to recede. As the flood ebbed away, the two who had been sacrificed emerged, changed forever to pillars of stone, facing west across the plains of Zuni.

When at last the land became good to walk upon and the people were able to descend to the valley, they were very happy for their trials had been great. They built anew the Town of the Middle and called it Halóna Ítiwana (Halóna, the midmost); but the desolated part they called Halónawan because they had erred there.

Although the earth no longer rumbled, the fathers of the people questioned in their hearts, fearing further misfortune if they had still erred in the resting-place for their sacred fetishes. So they devised a means whereby this might be checked. When the sun reached the middle between winter and summer they brought out the things of lightning and earthquake, and even summoned the keepers of the great shell who were skilled in magic. Then, as is done now, the people fasted and all fires were close kept and for ten days they made ready. On the last night the great shell was laid by the fire in the Kiva of the North and watched throughout the night by its keepers, the clan elders, and the Priests of the Bow. Although the awesome chants learned at Hán'thlipíngkia were sung, yet the earth only rumbled deeply and afar, but did not tremble nor did the dread seven cause destruction, only storms. Then the priests gave thanks and new fires were lighted after the old were cast out as a new year began for the Zuni resting at the stable Middle of the World.

Notes: 1 Genesis

In the story of Genesis the myth is a curious blend of Christian and Native-American beliefs for it postulates the creation of the cosmos from an endless dark void by an omniscient being, a very biblical concept. However, the being then transforms himself into the Sun Father, a purely native personage. As the Zuni Sun Father, he first creates the great encircling waters upon which the Zuni world is to float (Bunzel 1933, 187, 192) and then forms the Earth Mother and the Sky Father, a singular exception to most Pueblo beliefs. Usually the Sun is considered to be a man who, though possessing great powers, has many of the frailties of human beings (Parsons 1939, x, 258); or is the secondary creation of men, constructed of cloth, paint, and wood (ibid., 212). The only other legend giving the Sun the powers of a creator is found among the Hopi of Third Mesa. This myth attributes the contents of the world to a joint creative effort by the Sun and Huruing Wuhti, Goddess of Hard Substances, or in another version of the myth, by the Sun and Kokyang Wuhti, the Spider Grandmother (Voth 1905, 5). Courlander also attributes to Tawa, the Hopi Sun God, the role of a creator, when as a male force he impregnates the female earth and gives rise to growing things (Courlander 1971, 205). However this is fertilization rather than creation. In actuality the myth Courlander (ibid., 17–18) records from First Mesa has been strongly affected by the Zuni influence there and duplicates Cushing's folktale of the Sky Father impregnating the Earth Mother, the only change being the substitution of the Sun Father for the Sky Father who is not present at Hopi. In addition the Hopi personalize the earth as a male, Muyingwa.

The most widespread stories of the Sun Father concern his function as the "Holder of the Roads" or the fates of men. As such he receives prayers for health, happiness, longevity, and continuation, albeit he also promotes fertility and functions as a warrior. In Cushing's myth the designation of the world as an Earth Mother may be esoteric as it is not a thought held by the general populace. The Zuni say, "The earth is not a being" (Parsons 1917, 251, n.7).

Inherent in the nature of the first supernal beings is their ability to transmute, to change their shape from one form to another regardless of dimensions. Thus the Sky Father and the Earth Mother talk to one another in the manner of human parents. This concept of metamorphism is a basic tenet in most Native-American religious thinking where all beings (plants, animals, insects, natural objects) possess the power of change and may shift from one form to another depending upon their need and environment. It is a concept most easily likened to our perception of the three states of water where circumstance and environment dictate whether it is a gas, liquid, or solid. The Pueblo apply this concept to all things and believe, in addition, that it is self-determined. In this world of shifting forms, only social organization provides order.

Notes: 2 Formation of the World

The question posed and answered by the Earth Mother is how shall their children know one place from another? Her answer makes it apparent that it is not the physical attributes of the land alone that she is describing but rather the way in which mankind will determine their land holdings. This visualization springs from the manner in which native people orient themselves within their environment. Ask directions of an urbanite and all of the data given will start with markers at the periphery of the known and focus inward toward the goal, a centripetal concept. Ask the same question of one who has lived all his life in open undivided country and the answer will begin with, "You are here," and will then direct you outward toward the horizon, a centrifugal view. The Earth Mother's visualization is the latter. Perceived from the vantage point of the home village, the land extends away to the serrated mountains on the horizon like the interior of a great bowl, almost as stylized as the terraced asperging bowl used by the priests in the kiva to represent the land. All Pueblo territory is perceived in this manner with the important "terraced mountains", those in the cardinal directions, being emphasized (Stephen 1936; Voth 1905; Ortiz 1969).

Above these terraced mountains the clouds rise in the summer and gather in the winter. The rush of warmer air from the valleys up the slopes of the mountains to condense in clouds in the colder air of the higher elevations is an event noted by every inhabitant in the Southwest. The spontaneous appearance of clouds bespeaks of the supernatural to the scientifically unsophisticated. Clouds are then the froth made by the Earth Mother and borne aloft by the breath of supernaturals and dead children.

A duplication of the Earth Mother's actions is to be found in most of the Keresan pueblos and at Zuni where foam is made to imitate clouds in rain ceremonials (Stevenson 1904, 173–178). The ritual involves filling a terraced bowl with medicine water and then adding powdered yucca root which contains a strong saponin. When the water is whipped it produces a heavy lather that foams up and over the sides of the bowl. The froth is caught and lifted off to be cast to the cardinal directions, placed on various altars, or put upon the heads and bodies of priests, priestesses, and other leaders (Parsons 1939, 376). Among the Keresan Pueblos such as Santo Domingo and San Felipe it is quite often the women who make the froth to imitate the clouds (ibid., 132, n.*). At Cochiti the women who perform this ritual are referred to as *shiwanna* or thunderclouds (Stevenson 1894, 76 ff.).

Cushing's legend of the Zuni Sky Father making and placing the stars is not a typical Pueblo myth but is seemingly unique. The flavor of the story is in fact much more characteristic of tales from the eastern Woodland Indians. Most Pueblo myths personalize the more important stars and attribute the placement of the others to accident or carelessness. The most common Zuni tale recounts that the stars are parts of ancient monsters thrown into the sky by the War Twins (Parsons 1939, 213). Among the Hopi it is a careless act of Coyote who spilled the jar full of stars, scattering them about rather than placing them carefully in position (Cushing 1923, 144). In Zuni, it is Bitsitsi, a patron of the Néwekwe Society, who makes the Milky Way by flinging a handful of ashes across the night sky (Bunzel 1932b, 917). The more prominent stars or planets like the Morning or Evening Star are perceived as supernatural being with duties such as serving as the Warriors of the Sun (Cushing 1896, 384). It would seem that the portion of the myth in which the Sky Father makes and places the stars is an addition, possibly from elsewhere, tacked on to give symmetry to the tale.

Notes: 3 Birth of the Twins

Myths concerning the appearance of two small deities known as the Little War God Twins are found from Mexico to the Great Plains and throughout this region their form and function remain relatively the same. Everywhere they are beings who guide and instruct, who cope with that which is beyond the ability of man. They are a liaison between mankind and his gods. They are teachers who educate through object lessons both good and bad. Although the Two Little War Gods are diminutive and often thought of as irresponsible children delighting in the dreadful, they are yet mighty warriors capable of splitting the earth, carving great canyons, destroying monsters, and in general assisting mankind. They bring with them the cold and occasionally, misfortune. But their most notable characteristic is their innate ability to harden things, inuring against hardships, strengthening the hearts of warriors, making the surface of the earth solid, and even turning people to stone. The symbol of their capabilities as warriors is the pointed skull cap worn by each of the twins.

There is a general belief among Pueblo people that the Sun begets all twins. In addition the Hopi and Zuni impute any twin birth to either contact with animals like deer or antelope which consistently bear twins, or to dual conception (Eggan 1950, 48). In the latter instance it is believed that one child is conceived during the daylight hours by the sun and the other at night by man (Parsons 1939, 204). In consequence all twins, including the War God Twins, are spoken of as children of the Sun.

At Zuni there are at least two myths that tell of the birth of the Two Little War Gods. One is a generalized story, more common among the Hopi, which relates that the War Gods are the result of a maiden impregnated first by a sunbeam and then by rainwater, the elder twin being Child of the Sun and the younger Child of Water (Stephen 1929, 8). The other tale, more specific to Zuni, recounts their appearance from the foam of a waterfall following a freshet (Bunzel 1932a, 525). Cushing's myth is similar except that it gives their birthplace as the foam on the Great Waters upon which the earth rests rather than from a flood upon its surface. The white-peaked skull cap the War Gods wear represents the foam from which they sprang and similar hats are worn by Zuni warriors and war priests (Cushing 1882 [1970, 38]). The cap is found not only among the Zuni but also among the Hopi and Keresan peoples as well (Stephen 1936, 765) and occasionally among the Navajo (Franciscan Fathers 1910, 461, fig. 3).

Among the devices given the Twin War Gods by their Sun Father was a fog-making shield that would turn all weapons and yet let the rain drop through (Cushing 1896, 4). Believed to have been spun from clouds and wind-driven spray, the shield could both hide and defend the Two (ibid., 382). Because the shield was made from the clouds which support the Sky Ocean upon which rests the Sky World, just as the earth is supported by its underlying ocean of waters and clouds, it possessed the power of floating. When turned upward the shield rose and if reversed it sank downward (ibid. 1892, 52, n.1). The shields could be used to go up or down depending upon which side the Twins sat or could make them invisible when the shields were placed over their heads (ibid., 1892, 52).

The Zuni make a miniature replica of this magic shield, usually accompanied by a tiny bow representing the great Cloud Bow with small arrows for the flint-tipped lightning carried by the War Gods. The small shield (*pialawe*) is made of a simple hoop of wood a few inches in diameter with an open mesh of cotton cord simulating clouds, radiating from a common center, plus an olivella shell or two. These shields are symbols of the Two Little War Gods as much as the pointed caps and are placed as prayer offerings in various shrines by the Priesthood of the Bow. Likewise the small shields, bows and arrows are placed in the shrine to the Áhaiyuta atop Dówa Yálanne (Corn Mountain) when the War God images are set out there (Stevenson 1904, Pl. XXXVIII). They may also be attached to stakes about four feet in length and set upright in cairn shrines atop hills that are connected in some manner with the War Gods (Fewkes 1892, 11).

Further to the west the Hopi call the miniature shield *pachaiyanpi*, a rain wheel or rain sieve, and believe that the deities may drop rain through it. The small bows are not used with the shields but were formerly offered by the War Chiefs at winter solstice rites (Parsons 1939, 305) as they were in Acoma, Laguna, and Santo Domingo. Either bows and arrows or the netted shields were offered to the sun during the winter solstice ceremony at all of the above pueblos as well. At San Felipe they were offered later in the spring during the ground preparation ceremony and also at Isleta (ibid., 1939, 305). In Acoma the small shield is an offering to all of the Kopishtaiya or supernaturals (White 1932, Pl. 15). Both Oraibi and Isleta chiefs, and at Jemez, the War Chief, put down a similar netted ring but without the bow and arrows as a "sandstorm shutter" to prevent wind or sand damage to the crops (Parsons 1925, 102). The placing of these small offerings is a practice that reaches far back in time, as miniature bows and arrows that are almost identical with those of the Zuni have been found in ceremonial context in the Upper Gila dwellings (Hough 1914, 99–102) from a period believed to have lasted from 900 to 1000 A.D.

Notes: 4 The First World

All of the Pueblo people in the Southwest have an Emergence myth, a tale of leaving an underworld that was evil or unsatisfactory for a better one beyond the sky. Their ways of reaching the sky, of penetrating it, and the location of their point of emergence into the upper world, are as varied as the people. But within the universal legend there are other limited categories of belief. One school of thought, held by the Keresans and the Zuni, holds that there were four previous worlds before entering this one. The Hopi, Tiwa, Tewa, and Towa postulate only two worlds, an underworld and the present one. (It is interesting to note that the Hopi are slowly assimilating the Keresan/Zuni concept of four worlds).

Both the Zuni and the Keresans detail their four Underworlds. Among the Keresans a specific color is assigned to each world beginning with yellow for the first world. The next is blue-green, the third is red, and the fourth is white. The current world was dark until the Sun was placed and then it became all colors (White 1962, 10). Distinctively the Zuni characterize their Underworlds by conditions and by increasing light rather than color.

The Zuni term for these worlds is *téhuli*, translated by Cushing as womb, world, or cave-world (Cushing 1896, 83). Bunzel adds understanding of the word when she points out that it is derived from *téhulikwin*, a dark enclosed space or an "inside space" (Bunzel 1932a, 488, n. 16). The first space or *téhuli* is totally without light, black as soot from which it takes its name. The second world where there is a faint lessening of the gloom is named Moss World, the third where the light is like faint starshine is called Mud World. The last is Wing World for the sun's rays are visible even though the Morning Star still shines. Cushing gives a bit of additional information in his alternative names wherein he links the four underworlds to the stages of conception and birth and accounts for his use of the term womb for the underworlds. This association does not seem to be present in the later accounts of Parsons and Bunzel.

The four stages that correspond to the underworlds are the Place of First Formation (conception), the Place of Gestation (located somewhere near the umbilicus), the Place of Sex Generation (vagina), and the fourth the Womb of Parturition, the Ultimate Uncoverable (birth). The fifth world is one of full daylight, as opposed to the dark world of the Keresans and the Hopi. Cushing calls it the World of Disseminated Light and Knowledge or Seeing, where the Zuni still live (Cushing 1896, 381–83). Parsons (1939, 219) lists the four worlds as Soot World, Sulphur-Smell-Inside World or Raw Dust World, Fog World, and Wing-Inner World, yet she also refers to the second world as the Moss World as does Bunzel.

Notes: 5 The Daylight World

Emergence myths such as this one are fertile ground for psychological interpretations or philosophical conjectures about the nature of the people who produced them. Yet it must be borne in mind that most of the stories are an amalgam containing elements from neighbors and from refugees of Spanish conflicts, and that there are within a single people both sacred and secular versions of the same myth.

Belief in emergence from an earth composed of several layers is found throughout Middle America, the Southeast, and the Southwest. Few of these legends, however, give such an uncomplimentary view of their progenitors as is given in Cushing's version of the Zuni Emergence myth. Nevertheless this view is repeated in the independent reports of Stevenson, Parsons, Bunzel, and others. Its closest parallel is the Keresan myth in which the people lived in dark and crowded underworlds and made their way upward to emerge into an unlit world, pale and soft as newborn children (Parsons 1939, 242).

The Zuni are unusual also in their place of emergence. The majority of Pueblo peoples trace their origins to a place identified by the Keresans as Shípapolima, a town lying deep in a lake or in a land of mists, while for the Hopi it becomes the Sipapu, an opening through a spring into the Underworld. For the Zuni, somewhat like the Hopi, it is a water-filled opening (Jimit'kianap-kiatea) far to the northwest, but one that drained so the Áshiwi could emerge and then as quickly refilled (Stevenson 1904, 26, 407).

For the Zuni the morning and evening stars are, in varying ways, thought of as attendants of one of their major deities, the Sun, announcing his arrival or departure and guarding his path. At the same time these two stars or planets are associated with war and as such are at times identified as the War God Twins (Parsons 1925, 126). Morning Star, in particular among the Tewa, is considered to be a messenger of the Sun or his War Chief (Parsons 1939, 205). In this particular myth Morning Star serves as the Sun's messenger to the newly emerged people rather than as one of the War Twins.

Notes: 6 The Winter and Summer People

Inherent in Pueblo thinking is the accounting for idiosyncracies, anomalous events, and most importantly for origins of social structure, by projecting all of them into the mythological past. Thus myths serve to mirror existing people, their beliefs and motivations. They offer validation for events and actions by attributing these to ancestors when in actuality the myths are explanations of contemporary life (Eggan 1950, 214). Consequently a myth has validity only for the time when it is told, for it is explaining existing conditions. However, myths bearing on the same subject but recorded at different times will form a rudimentary history of the people producing them. The legend which tells of the Zuni being divided into the Winter and Summer People not only explains the present through terms of the past but is also indicative of a shifting social structure.

To understand why the Zuni should have had a legend in 1881 explaining their division into two parts when they are not now so divided, requires a little historical perspective, some cultural anthropology as well as a bit of archaeology and philosophy.

Historically at the time of the Spanish Entrada, in 1540, the Zuni occupied seven villages: Mátsaki, Kyakime, Háwikuh, K'yánawe, Hámpasawan, Ke'tchina, and Halóna, the present town of Zuni, New Mexico. According to the description of one Mota Padilla (Hodge 1937, 55) of that first encounter: "They reached Tzibola (Cibola), which was a village divided into two wards." It is not known whether this referred to an architectural or social division, but in either instance it indicates that at least the village of Háwikuh (Tzibola) was in 1540 composed of two parts.

In the years following, from 1540 until 1680, the continuing pressures of the Spanish forced the abandonment of one Zuni village, Háwikuh, and culminated in the Zuni joining in the Pueblo-wide revolt of 1680. When the conquering Spaniards returned in 1696 the people of the six Zuni villages fled to a refuge atop Dówa Yálanne (Corn Mountain) and built a single large village. At this new location on the mountain the village was built in six architectural blocks, undoubtedly representing the six valley villages. There is no indication that any of the blocks were themselves divided in half nor that the entire village formed two wards, nor is there documentation of their social organization for this period. When at last the Zuni were persuaded to come down from their mountain refuge in the 1700s, the constant raiding by the neighboring Athapascans prevented their re-occupying the separate settlements and forced them instead to remain in a single defensible village, Halóna with its six kivas, the Zuni of today.

A century and a half later Cushing arrived to study the Zuni. During his stay, which began in autumn of 1879 and lasted through the winter of 1881, he uncovered data to show the ways in which the Zuni of that era conceptually divided themselves. He perceived that they were systematized along secular, fraternal, social, and sacred lines (Cushing 1920, 126–28). In the secular he pointed out that there were fraternities and cults controlling curing, warfare, rain-making, hunting, which were also separate organizing principles. In the social segment he listed all of the known clans, both existing and extinct, by name and indicated the presence of a phratral or linked clan system. In the sacred context he showed how the clans and fraternities were related to the six ceremonial structures, the *kíwitsin*, or kivas, of the Zuni, and how they interacted. He pointed out how each of the kivas and its members were characterized by particular attitudes and associations. He also noted that each kiva was always linked with a single direction and had its own definitive color as well as a cluster of natural phenomena, plants, and animals who shared perceived affinities. Interaction of the six kivas as a cooperating unit reinforced tribal unity as well as being the focal point of the four-part organizational system.

In addition Pueblo cosmology holds the belief that all aspects of nature, including mankind, belong to one great system of related life, a belief affirmed by both Cushing and Bunzel for the Zuni. The ordering of this convoluted cosmos is further complicated by its division into two halves of opposing nature, a completely dipolar world.

At its very inception, as Cushing's legend relates, mankind, creatures, and all things were created from the cohabitation of a cold Sky Father and a warm Earth Mother and were forever categorized by their inherent attributes as belonging with one or the other deity in an unending series of associations. Cushing's legend shows a recognition of this belief by the conceptual division of the Zuni into two halves or moieties. The Summer People, those of the Earth Mother, were the ones whose understanding and duties encompassed the sun, water, seeds, and fire and who used the kivas of the south, zenith, and nadir. The Winter People's functions and knowledge related to game animals, wild foods, ice, freezing, and hardness. They used the remaining three kivas of the north, west, and east.

Even in Cushing's time this moiety system existed only in legend and by inference, from the phratral organization Cushing described but which he believed showed obvious signs of weakening (Cushing 1920, 128). The changes in the Zuni lifeway since Cushing's time have been very extensive. Not only have the functions and duties relating to the activities of winter and summer disappeared but their mythological presence is diminishing as well. Nevertheless, the innate conservatism of Zuni thinking has retained the feeling of "rightness" in certain associations such as kivas and directions or groups of people linked by a common purpose.

Notes: 7 Origins of Clans and Societies

A clan is a unit of kinship. At Zuni it is composed of a named group of people who trace their common ancestry through the female line, a matrilineal system. Furthermore each clan has a fetish unique to it, an object which is considered to be the very essence, the seed or germ of some particular aspect of the environment such as an animal, a plant, or a natural force. This object, the "heart" of the clan, has great potency which must be preserved. Its safeguarding is of primary importance, and at the same time it must be prevented from harming the uninitiated. It is from this object or what it represents that the clan derives its name.

The clan also possesses and houses the ceremonial "tools" or ritual paraphernalia that have accumulated through generations of handling the fetish in varying ways, as well as possessing a cadre of individuals versed in its handling. These individuals are organized into four primary societies that attend the needs of the people: the Warriors, the Hunters, the Curers, and the Teachers. The harsher activities of war and hunting are associated with the Winter People while those of curing, teaching, or rain-making belong to Summer. In addition to these societies there are cults, groups of men who possess specific knowledge of chants, prayers, and other ceremonial activities that must be passed on intact to the younger ceremonialists.

Formerly the clan had a tendency to occupy that portion of the village which lay in the direction most often associated with its fetish and to hold ceremonies in a kiva appropriate to that direction and function.

More often than not several clans will have parallel or similar functions; for example, the Sun, Sky, and Eagle clans all relate to the Above or some aspect of it. Their functional relationship is recognized by the Zuni who feel that they are "linked". These clusters, larger than clans but smaller than moieties, are known as phratries, a system organized on function rather than kinship.

The roles of male and female also affect the clan, for the hearth and children belong to the women but to the men belong the cosmos and the mechanics to make it work. In consequence those functions relating to permanence, stability, safety, and continuation are the women's sphere while those of unpredictability, change, religion, warfare and curing are the men's. In consequence it is the women who care for and house the fetish of the clan but it is the men who use it.

The intermeshing systems of the Zuni seem to have answers for all contingencies so that the community should remain stable yet studies indicate that this is not the case. In the seventy-five year interval between Cushing's visit from 1879 to 1884 and Eggan's study in 1950, the Zuni have undergone enormous social change. Only myths and a sense of rightness recall the moiety organization. The phratries which Cushing felt were possibly weakening (Cushing 1920, 128) have completely disappeared. Even the clans have been immensely reduced in both number and importance (Eggan 1950, 200) as the Zuni base shifts from clan to household to reach equivalence with the dominant culture that surrounds it.

Notes: 8 Hardening of the World

The Zuni are almost alone in their tale of the Twins hardening the soft new world. Although the one attribute most consistently ascribed to the Two Little War Gods is their ability to strengthen objects, it is only at Zuni or among their immediate neighbors where this is applied to the world.

To the west the Hopi have tales in which the War Gods impart endurance and hardihood to men, and others that have the Two solidifying the world with their coldness. Courlander (1971, 26) relates a tale wherein the Two War Gods discuss the unfinished nature of the new land into which the Hopi have emerged. They decide that the land is too much the same, flat and muddy throughout, and that it should be dry with some relief to the level plain. Thereupon they set out to change the world by piling up mountains of mud and cutting canyons to carry the water away. Then they dry the land and harden it by playing *nahoydadatsia*, or stick ball, across the land. This tale, while undoubtedly Hopi in its details, is inconsistent with the other Hopi emergence myths related by such early ethnographers as Voth, Fewkes, Mindeleff, Parsons, Curtis, and Stephen who do not mention this theme. Quite possibly the Courlander tale is a recent Zuni importation incorporated into Hopi oral literature.

The tale does not appear to the east of Zuni or else is overridden by legends of a great flood or a story of emergence through a lake. Another group of legends, more typical of the eastern Pueblos, relates to the War Gods draining the land by carving mighty canyons to carry the water away.

Notes: 9 The Meeting of the Seed Peoples

In the manner of most Pueblo storytelling, advice that is believed to be pertinent for the contemporary listener is incorporated into a myth or legend, although frequently it has little bearing on the story line. In this instance the addition concerns the stubbornness of some of the people in not listening to their chiefs and refusing to continue on with the tribe, believing that they could survive alone. This small extraneous vignette is added to the myth as advice to the people who are being told the story. Strength in numbers and cooperation were facts of life for the Zuni in 1880, hammered home by the depredations of Spanish, Navajo, and Apache neighbors, a lesson undoubtedly repeated many times over and given even greater validity by attaching it to a mythological happening.

The ancient Zuni or Áshiwi in that legendary meeting reacted in the manner of nomadic peoples the world over, where a quick attack offers the advantage in the immediacy of a physical threat. The Seed People, on the other hand, were settled and having more to lose, chose the diplomatic or non-violent solution. The two widely different tribes met, of course, at the epitome of sacred locations, Shípapolima, the lace of Mists.

Shípapolima, or Shípap, is the place where Mankind emerged from the Underworld in the belief of all the Keresan peoples (Parsons 1939, 182). The more east-

123

ern pueblos, however, believe that they emerged through lakes, and to the west the opening for the Hopi was a spring, their Sipapu (Voth 1905, 10). But for all Pueblo people it is the place, the one where supernatural events or the most important happenings always occur, where great lessons are learned or valuable ceremonies secured.

The incipient conflict is settled by the ultimate Pueblo contest of using religious paraphernalia to produce results indicating who is in the right. In the myth the Zuni are apparently unfamiliar with the process and they have to be argued into trying it. The rewards of this contest are presented in terms of mutual benefit but may possibly represent an outnumbered group buying its way out of a predicament.

Notes: 10 The First-Growing-Grass Clan

The ritual contest between the First-Growing-Grass clan and the People of the Dew contains the very embodiment of Pueblo belief, particularly as represented in Zuni a century ago. That concept is that like produces like. Their hope was for rain and new soil to produce the desired crop. Thus the objects chosen for the ceremony were things that occur naturally with new soil and rain.

In all farming cultures there is a strong emphasis on seeds. Often the concept of seeds is expanded to include many things that might not occur to the outsider. The germination and growth of seeds was used as a model for such things as the weather, springs, and even Pueblo villages. Towns were embodied with roots, a stem, flowers, and seeds. For a new town to come into being, it had to be "plant-ed" with seed people. The extension of this idea made it possible to plant a spring by assembling the proper ingredients. Because certain creatures and plants are always found where there is water, in this inverse logic it stands to reason that if you have the creatures you will eventually get the water. The "seeds" in this instance are tadpoles, moss, cattails, and the like. Undoubtedly there were other similar things which represented the "seeds" of new soil and other desired elements that would be used to produce the desired result.

Those who gathered to begin the trial are those who would have been con-

125

sidered essential in Zuni a century ago. They would have been the leaders of the village political system from the House of Houses, all of the elder cult members who care for the ritual paraphernalia and know by heart the chants and prayers necessary for a fraternity or medicine society ceremony, as well as the priests of the Néwekwe Society and the chiefs of the Corn clan who consecrate and care for all the important seed crops of the Zuni.

Any important ceremony, such as this one, requires a retreat wherein all the participants sequester themselves in appropriate locations for a specified period of time. Here they remain, depriving themselves of food, water, salt, sleep, and sex to purify their minds. It was a time used for meditation and praying and the preparation of prayer sticks to carry their message to the beings who controlled that which they desired.

The mythic ceremony performed that night is the same as the one every farmer followed during Cushing's stay. As he reports in The Millstone:

> . . . . He has infused the consciousness of his
> prayer into the plumed stick; that with his sacred
> cigarette he has prepared a way 'like the trails of the
> winds and rains' [clouds] for the wafting of that prayer
> to the gods of all regions. That having taken the
> cloud-inspiring down of the turkey, the
> strength-giving plume of the eagle, the water-loving
> feather of the duck, the path-finding tails of the birds
> who counsel and guide summer; having moreover
> severed and brought hither the flesh of the
> water-attracting tree, . . . (*Zuni Breadstuff.* Indian
> Notes and Monographs v. VIII, Museum of the
> American Indian. Heye Foundation, New York. 1920.)

This prayer stick is imbedded in the exact center of a field that the farmer has constructed of many small catchment basins which will retain both the flood water and the new soil it carries, depositing it for the benefit of his crop. Before placing the prayer feather he makes an equal-armed cross of cornmeal drawn on the ground to represent the cardinal directions. The prayer feather is then placed where the lines intersect. At the tip of each of the lines a hole is poked deep into the soil and a kernel of corn of the proper color is dropped into it. On the left of the north hole another is made to represent the Zenith and one to the right of the south hole to represent the Nadir (Cushing 1920, 177).

During the night when the seven great stars rose, they were not those of the Big Dipper or the Pleiades but instead were those of Orion. The rectangle which forms the Hunter's body is composed of brilliant stars, all but one being of first or second magnitude and even that one is of third magnitude (Zim and Baker 1956, 90–92). The three others that lead into the square are the three bright stars of Orion's belt perceived as being a line perpendicular to the rectangle. Far brighter than the stars of the Big Dipper, those of Orion and the Pleiades are best known to the Pueblo people. They are markers used to time the beginning of many nighttime ceremonies. For others the three stars of Orion's belt are Winter stars while those of the Pleiades are the Summer stars (Bunzel 1932a, 487). The Pleiades are also spoken of as the Seed Stars and are believed to represent the seven Corn Maidens.

The rectangle of brilliant stars is seen as the four directions and Orion's belt as the line of the Zenith, Nadir, and Middle. This symbolism is transferred to the field of the Zuni farmer wherein each kernel of corn planted on the figure drawn in the soil represents a star in the constellation. Even as the Sun Father held the gleaming sparks of stars which are the seeds of Heaven in his palm during the formation of the world, so does the Zuni farmer place the first kernels of corn in his field.

Notes: 11 The People of the Dew

The importance of corn, the staple food for all Southwestern tribes, cannot be overstated. It is behind most ceremonies. Countless ritual acts are devoted to it and taboos and proscripted behavior guard it, thus binding all humans into patterns of respect for this major food source. It is far easier to meet these countless demands if the recipients are thought of as human beings or at least of human origin rather than plants or some austere and distant being. Failure of the crops can be endured with greater patience if the crops are thought of as Corn Maidens fleeing rather than plants dying from some unassignable cause (Parsons 1939, x).

The corn or maize used by the Pueblo people occurs in a variety of colors, of which six or seven are customarily used for ceremonies. In the same familiar pattern each is associated with a particular direction, and at Zuni, with a kiva. Thus yellow corn represents the north, blue corn the west, red the south, and white the east. Mixed corn is assigned to the zenith and dark purple or black corn indicates the nadir. Sweet corn is often chosen to represent the middle or center of these directions. Each type of corn is anthropomorphized as a Corn Maiden.

Cushing's myth relates how these Corn Maidens came into being. The tale is related in fanciful terms and yet, as is so often true with his information, it contains interesting parallels with existing ceremonies. It is always difficult to separate a tale, which in actuality is a statement explaining current practices, from a myth that has temporal depth. In this instance there are circumstances that indicate considerable antiquity.

Among the Hopi to the west many of the women belong to a society called the Mamzrau or Marau which holds a ceremony each fall during harvest time. The purpose of the society is to promote fertility and growth in both humans and crops (Voth 1912). At intervals this society performs a different type of dance than their usual give-away performance in the "Knee-High" dance. It is one that is known as the Palhik'o Mana or Water-Drinking-Girls dance (Titiev 1944, 124–5, 165, 168). Although the ceremony varies between mesas it is essentially a dance by six women wearing enormous tabletas who appear with a single male in a style that is almost identical with the myth of the Corn Maidens' origin as related by Cushing for the Zuni. The women's growth ceremonial at Zuni, the Thla'hewe or Corn Dance, is quite similar, although the paraphernalia differs slightly.

While it is possible for the myth to have been an explanation of the ceremony rather than a tale with historical depth at Zuni, the same cannot be said for the dance at Hopi. In the latter instance two possibilities exist: either the Palhik'o Mana was copied from the Thla'hewe at Zuni and added to the Mamzrau ceremony or, what is more likely, it was always a part of a growth ceremony from which both the Hopi and Zuni forms sprang.

The Hopi received the Mamzrau when it was introduced by the priestess of the society who was captured and brought from Awatovi to Walpi during the disturbance there in 1703. How and when it reached Awatovi is not known although there is a strong possibility that it was brought by the peripatetic Badger clan who dallied for a while in Mátsaki before moving on to Awatovi. In any case the presence of the Mamzrau with its attendant Palhik'o Mana performance seemingly indicates an origin time prior to the Spanish Entrada as archaeological evidence indicates that Mátsaki was abandoned very close to that time period. Supplementary data from the myths of the Badger clan support the archaeology that indicates movement of people between these two villages. It is noteworthy that the Badger clan is included in the myth of the origin of the Corn Maidens in Cushing's version.

Notes: 12 The Blessing of the Deities

Once the seven corn plants have been magically produced, their human counterparts or representatives, the seven maidens, must be transformed from humans to supernaturals and three deities are chosen to accomplish this sanctification. They are: a flute-playing divinity, a being who is represented by a medicine plant, and one who figures strongly in the Zuni winter solstice ceremony.

The choice of Paíyatuma, the flute-player, as the godfather to the Corn Maidens is unexpected, for many of his attributes and duties seem at variance with what is required. He is a known seducer of maidens (Parsons 1939, 204) and the patron of the Néwekwe, a Zuni society whose members are noted for their behavior as clowns, as gluttons capable of eating anything, and as profligate parodists of everything. In myths set later in time it is Paíyatuma's followers, the Flute Youths, who drove the Corn Maidens into hiding by attempting to make free with their persons. Later still it is also Paíyatuma, in his role as stern Bitsitsi, who finds the Corn Maidens and returns them to the starving Zuni from whom they had fled because of their disrespectful treatment by the Flute Youths. He is also the protagonist of the Flute ceremony, a performance that parallels in form and content that of the Corn Maidens but is designed to produce moisture (Cushing 1896, 435). It was the disrespect to the Corn Maidens shown by the Zuni, who delighted in this new Flute ceremony to the exclusion of the Corn ceremony, that almost lost the maidens forever.

Possibly the best clue to the role of Paíyatuma as godfather of the Corn Maidens may lie in his position as First Youth or Sun Youth. In the early world he played his flute, the young men sang, and the Corn Maidens ground corn. The songs were prayers for the return of warmth and vegetation (Parsons 1939, 452). However, as the son of the Sun, Paíyatamu is also the God of Dawn and morning moisture or Dew, the elements of early light and moisture that are deemed necessary to the growth of corn. But he is also the child of the Earth Mother (Bunzel 1933, 249), the giver of corn. As one of the three deities in the myth, Paíyatuma, in conferring the gift of corn, undoubtedly represents none other than the Underground Mother. His blessing confers immortality on the Corn Maidens and eminence on those who guard the seed while at the same time warning of dire consequences for disrespect to them.

The deity, Ténatsali, whom Cushing calls the God of Time and Directions, represents a medicine plant. (Ténatsali is also the Zuni name given to Cushing and is translated as "Medicine Flower"). One of the properties of this unidentified plant is that its flowers change color with age. Consequently the name "God of Time" seems appropriate for it. It is further distinguished by the succession of colors found in the flowers, new and old, that duplicate those associated with the cardinal directions for the Zuni (Stevenson 1904, 192). This attribute undoubtedly produced the name "God of Directions". The plant is used, among other things, to heal wounds and by inference would be used to assure the renewal of the substance of the Corn Maidens through the passage of time.

Kwélele, the dark partner of Shi'tsukia in the winter solstice, continues the ripening of the corn through the dark hours. He is the opposite of Paíyatuma and with the fire that he carries in his torch he brings the corn to maturity just as the fires of the Hopi Masau-u were used to ripen his corn before the Sun was placed in the sky. In addition Kwélele's torch confers hardness to the kernels of corn as they ripen.

Notes: 12 The Blessing of the Deities

Notes: 13 The Search for the Middle

Up to this point the stage has been set by explaining the origins of the deities and their roles, by telling how the people were organized into priest and layman, clan, moiety, and society, and by recounting how corn came into being.

In this sequence, concerning Ka'wimosa's children, the Áshiwi or Zuni are located geographically and the origins of some of their more important kachinas related. The locale for these events and places is in Arizona, northwest of the small town of St. Johns, at the confluence of the Zuni and Little Colorado Rivers. It was here that the sacred lake, the Lake of Whispering Waters containing Kóthluwalawan, the Home of the Kachinas, was located before Anglo-American water use dried it. This is also where the dead came to join the kachinas in their underwater village.

Here also are the mountains, one to the north of the Zuni River where the Koyemshi live, and one to the south where their mother, Síwuluhsitsa, resides. These beings, the Koyemshi or Mudheads, are the interpreters, the husbands (in the sense of guardians) of the kachinas for they take care of their needs. It is the Koyemshi who, speaking with reverse intent, babbling nonsense and behaving like simpletons, may yet make a solemn announcement of what dance is being held, which kachinas will appear, and when. Despite their idiocy the Koyemshi are the most sacred of the Zuni divinities, neither gods nor kachinas but oracles of the ancients. The Zuni men who are asked to personify them have a very demanding job. Their role requires a year's commitment filled with prayers, songs, and actions that must be learned. Quantities of prayer sticks must be made then placed in locations both near and far; they must as well undergo fasting and other deprivations during the long retreats of the Koyemshi. The men who impersonate them are on call from other organizations within the pueblo who dance or perform other rituals. The people of Zuni may deny them nothing regardless of their request.

Notes: 14 The Separation of the Clans

In their search for "the Middle", the Zuni migration pattern appears to have been movement followed by the short occupation of a site to replenish food supplies and then movement again. The myth presents a clear picture of how the Zuni of one hundred years ago believed such a migration would have been structured. The clusters of related clans, the Winter, Summer, and Midmost People, would each have held a fetish unique to themselves but needed by the other segments of the Zuni tribe if all were to survive. It was an organization that could maximize use of the land by allowing each of the three groups to disperse and take advantage of natural resources and yet be able to recombine as a tribe, very much as the Great Basin tribes did into late historic times. Rather than being the tale of a journey, this myth is a historical statement about perceived tribal organization.

Today the Zuni pass out leaflets to visitors, based on non-Indian research, that indicate their early migration route as the Zuni believe it to be. It is very close to the myth related by Cushing. Beginning somewhere in northwestern Arizona, beyond the San Francisco Peaks and the Grand Canyon, the route crosses the Colorado River near the confluence of the Little Colorado River, where the Hopi emergence myth begins at their Sipapu. The route then continues upstream toward the headwaters of the Little Colorado on the western side, even though

135

Cushing's legend says all the rivers they came to ran from east to west, a situation that would put them on the east bank. At the junction of the Zuni River with the Little Colorado in east central Arizona, their migration route turns northeast. One thing is certain, the Zuni would have had a most difficult time dividing and following the northern, central, and southern valleys as related in the tale because all of the tributary valleys were at right angles to the postulated route until they crossed the Little Colorado and turned up the Zuni River. Regardless of the actual conformation of the land, the manner of traveling through the country, dividing, coming together again, is consistent with other aboriginal Pueblo travel.

It is, of course, impossible to tell whether the myth was tailored in Cushing's time to fit the known physical conditions of the region closest to Zuni or whether the myth is far more ancient and reflects a memory of movement through this particular location. Geographically almost all detail is missing until they reach this location. That it is an important area is apparent for it figures very strongly in Zuni religion and is visited at least quadrennially by the ceremonialists of Zuni who conduct religious rites at the former site of their sacred lake and its vanished Kóthluwalawan.

Notes: 15 The Abode of Souls

The crossing of the red river, wherein some children were lost, is more than a dangerous event in the journey of the Áshiwi. It marks a change in the tenor of the myths as well from one of speculative beginnings and vague locations to clearly identified locales. Also incorporated into the myths for the first time, with one or two exceptions, are the names and homes of divinities and other associated supernaturals other than the twin culture heroes, and the deities of sun, sky, and earth. This is where the kachinas originate and where the first sacred dance is performed. Here also is the entry to the home of the dead. It is also at this place that the Macaw clan and other Midmost clans, the very heart of the group, broke away from the main party of the Zuni to be lost forever in the southern lands.

Geographically, the home of the dead, the kachinas, and other supernaturals, was a small lake or lagoon known as Hátin-kiaiakwi or Listening Spring. It received this name because the water made a noise that sounded like the quiet whispering of unseen people when one listened to it. Other names for it may be translated as the Lake of the Ancients, or the Lake of Whispering Waters. It lay between two small mountains on the Zuni River, above its confluence with the Little Colorado River. With typical inelegance the mountains are now known as North Mountain and South Mountain and between them lies Stinking Spring.

The lake has long since dried up with the demands of contemporary water users but it retains its mystique for the Zuni who periodically weather the wrath of ranchers fearful for their gates and livestock, to make pilgrimages to it.

Mythically the lake had within it a six-chambered house known as Kóthlu-walawan or by the archaic name of Wenima. Herein resided the divinities and kachinas of the six directions, the dead who were finished with their mortal life and entitled to entry—the others perforce had to watch the dances through the windows (Stevenson 1904, 32). The children who were lost to the red waters drifted down into this mystic home to become the Council of the Gods, liaison between supernaturals and humans, or some say, the Kókokshi, the beautiful dancers.

Notes: 16, 17, 18 The Journeys of Kiaklo and How He Came Home

Kiaklo, the kachina, appears dressed all in white; even his body is painted white except for a strip from chest to navel (Bunzel 1932b, 872). In his right hand he carries a duck stuffed with seeds and cotton wearing a string of tiny shell beads about its neck. Across Kiaklo's forehead is an arc of rainbow colors flanked by black and white blocks in the band that represent the Milky Way (ibid., Pl. 28a). These stripes end in a red-fringed squash blossom over each ear. His eyes and mouth are mere black dots with three pendant lines under each. Every detail of his costume, paraphernalia, and appearance may be found in the recounting of his mythical wanderings.

When he comes to Zuni as a kachina his call is a shrill cry of "Kiaklo! Kiaklo! Kiaklo!" from whence comes his common name but the Koyemshi who bring him to Zuni on their shoulders call him by his personal name of Iwaiyahuna (Wright 1985, 50–54). He is respectfully called grandfather by the Zuni but he is a bustling, officious, self-important personage, somewhat ridiculous despite his great power (Bunzel 1932a, 522).

The function of Kiaklo in the village is of great importance even though he comes only once every four years. He is Páutiwa's speaker, the representative of the gods, who conveys a message from the supernatural world and relates the history of the Zuni during all of their travels. He speaks to the boys who are to be initiated and reiterates the codes of behavior that must be observed and the patterns of respect due the deities. He thereby insures that each intiate will be recognized by the deities as a breath relative to be aided in times of need. He is the initial step in inducting the boys into the kachina cult and reinforcing tribal mores and beliefs.

He enters Zuni borne on the back of the smallest Koyemshi he can find. Here the Koyemshi cluster about him to wheedle and sing to entice him into each of the six kivas. Once inside he delivers an oration that may last for six hours as he brings the words and benedictions of the deities. When all of the kivas have been visited he is again taken on the shoulders of the Koyemshi in a re-creation of the myth and carried from the village of Zuni toward distant Kóthluwalanne.

Notes: 19 The Return of the Brothers Ánahoho

Among the Zuni the exclamation, "Ána!" is one of distress. The name of these two kachinas, Ánahoho, means "to take away bad luck" (Bunzel 1932b, 994). Their figures are all white with a black handprint faintly outlined in red in the center of their faces. Two panels of the dance sash hang from the front of their waists and around their necks are either crow feathers or the entire bird. At either side of the head is a circle divided into six parts, each painted a different color. When these two kachinas come during the initiation of the boys, they accompany the white Sálimopia and are impersonated by some member of the Ohewa or Eastern Kiva, or someone appointed by the dance director of that kiva. The special prayers that they intone to remove bad luck are taught to them by an albino woman who has no other ceremonial connections. The constant reiteration of white means that these kachinas are either from the east or associated in some way with the attributes of it.

Their role when they come during initiation is to roam about the roof tops where anything in the way of a container is cast down into the streets to be totally destroyed by the Sálimopia and other kachinas. When the kachinas who are to whip the boys enter the six kivas to drink medicine that will excite them and harden them for the task ahead, the Ánahoho remain outside on the kiva roof (Wright

141

1985, 64). Undoubtedly this is because of their association with bad luck for, like all other kachinas they have power over certain attributes of the natural world. Thus they can cause bad luck as easily as they can remove it. When the boys are whipped the Ánahoho join in that part of the rite to exorcise bad luck.

Cushing's myth indicates that the function of these kachinas is to search for their brother Kiaklo and in the process destroy the containers that will accompany the dead to the Underworld. This has some interesting similarities to one of the prehistoric cultures to the south of Zuni, the Mimbres, who broke a hole in the bottom of their vessels when they were placed with a burial. Presumably this was to let the spirit escape or more likely to send the vessel to the Underworld with its owner.

Bunzel (1932b, 994) relates that the Ánahoho came to warn the Zuni of impending bad luck, which in one instance was an impending attack by the Navajo. The Navajo were ambushed and many were killed while none of the Zuni perished. The elder Ánahoho put his right hand in their blood and marked his face while his younger brother used his left hand and did the same, thereby affording a way of distinguishing the two. It is an interesting tale for it implies that the Ánahoho already existed with a specific role before they received their identifying mark. This probably represents an acceptable explanation where knowledge of the symbolic content of the handprint is unknown rather than a variant of the actual myth.

The Ánahoho of Zuni are present among the neighboring Hopi in two particular forms. One, the Pot-Carrier or Sivu-i-qiltaka (Colton 1959, 46), appears in the Mixed Dance. However, his head is black and the mark on his face is white with an outline of red. He carries a pot on his back supported by a tumpline and is followed by the Tulakin Mana or Stirring Girl. The only similarity is the mark on the face and the association with a pottery vessel. The second form of the Hopi kachina is that of Matya, "Pressed or Leaning Against" or Malachpeta, "Fingermarks". This form may come stripped as a runner wearing only a breechclout with his body painted blue and a black handprint on his face, or brown with a black handprint on his chest and a white handprint on a black head. In neither instance do these kachinas appear to have the role that Ánahoho has in Zuni for removing bad luck.

Notes: 20 The Great Journey Renewed

The legend that tells of the War Gods removing the Zuni's tails and separating their webbed fingers and toes is strangely out of position in their myths. It is always placed at Hán'thlipíngkia, after the crossing of the river where the children who fell into the river were changed, growing tails and webbed hands and feet. This is a contradiction since they should have already had these appendages. It also occurs after the origin of corn, where the People of the Dew asked for a boy perfect in form to participate in that ceremony. In content this particular legend belongs among the earliest events that transpire after the Zuni emerge from the Under-world. Its consistent setting at Hán'thlipíngkia indicates that it is a marker for an event of great significance, a preparation for something to come.

Notes: 21 The Twin War Gods
and the Origin of the Priests of the Bow

Belief in the Twins is a very widespread phenomenon for it covers the Southwest and reaches from the West Coast to far out in the Plains. Invariably these two are characterized as risk-takers, as beings who assist men in their direst need yet who are infantile in either attitude or appearance, and sometimes both. One of the Twins is older than the other and is often thought of as one individual with the echo or shadow of himself being the other Twin, a personified reflection. The relationship of the elder to the younger is similar in concept to the way a right-handed person views his left hand. Of their many attributes, one is the ability to harden things whether it is the soil, the nature of men, or the stringency of the weather. They are just as often portrayed as evil as they are good. Their behavior is that of juvenile delinquents and ranges from bedeviling their guardian Spider Grandmother to sly subservience in their approach to their father, the Sun. They appear to be governed by whim and directed by chance. Consequently it is of interest to find in Cushing's myth that the Twins were originally beneficent guides and caretakers of the Zuni, using their wisdom and powers only for good until the site of the ancient village of Hán'thlipíngkia is reached and they are then transformed. From this point onward they are truly War Gods, renamed and behaving in the manner of the Two Little War Gods of their neighbors, rather than the kindly elder brothers of earlier times.

Cushing, in describing the paraphernalia of the Twin War Gods after their transformation, presents an inventory of the arsenal available to the Zuni warrior, including items actually used in warfare and others used to determine or influence the course of future events. The weapons listed span both time and space, for the War Gods and their human counterparts, the Bow Priests, are equipped with bows and arrows in mountain lion skin quivers yet at the same time they hold in their hands the atlatl and spears used only in Basketmaker times or in the Valley of Mexico. Hung from their belts are the slings and pouches of stones also common to the warriors of Mexico, as well as the face-pulping wooden war club of the Pima and other river tribes of Arizona, and the ancient stone celt or *chamahia* of the prehistoric Pueblo people. Over their backs are the ubiquitous shields of the Pueblo tribes. The presence of fire-hardened skin body armor coupled with helmets made from the thick neck hide of an elk is not reflected in the armament of their neighbors except in the padded cotton war garments of the people far to the south and in the armor of the Spanish. Thus it would seem that Cushing's War Gods and their homologues, the Bow Priests, had knowledge of many types of weapons, more than could be carried by any single warrior. When the Bow Priest arms himself today he comes carrying bow and arrow with quiver, a short club, a helmet, shield, and buckskin cape. But in addition to these, the War Gods equipped themselves with the games upon which wagers are placed, like kick sticks and tethered balls. These are devices of divination to guess the future and influence the chances of men.

At the same time the War Gods are transformed, another group of supernaturals is introduced for the first time. These are the Chiefs of Directions, the beings who inhabit the mountains at the four corners of the world and reside at the ends of the Zenith and Nadir. They are the ultimate arbiters of the forces of nature such as the weather and earthquakes. In the Southwest the environment is such that the weather is distinctly different depending upon the direction from which it arises. To endow these forces with personae is inevitable and as such they exist in Acoma to the east and Hopi to the west. But their incomprehensibility and aloofness from humanity have in consequence prevented any impersonation of these beings. Only their power is recognized and named.

Notes: 22 War with the Black People

In most Zuni myths the participants have multiple names, ones that refer to their status within the tribe and others that are personal names. In consequence the Two War Gods are known collectively as the Áhaiyuta, a title referring to both divinities but usually referring only to the elder War God whose personal name is Úyuyewi. His brother, the younger War God, is called Mátsailema. In a similar fashion the female warrior of the Kianakwe is called Chákwaina Ókyatsiki by Cushing. Nowadays it is more commonly rendered Chakwaina Okya or Old Woman Warrior. Her personal name, however, is Kúyapalitsa.

It is very difficult to resist the temptation to try to name or locate the Kianakwe, whom the Zuni fought, because of their many distinctive traits noted in Cushing's myth. First they were a people related to the Ákakakwe, the Acomans, and hence a Keresan tribe. They wore long white cotton robes, the first the Zuni had seen (Stevenson 1904, 36), indicating they were relatively sophisticated in their crafts. They possessed knowledge of irrigation, methods that would transport both water and soil to their great fields, techniques not generally known in the Southwest. They built large houses on the heights near their fields. In addition to this they were not native to the region, their point of origin having been far to the south or southeast.

Interestingly Cushing presents only the barest outline of the story of the Kianakwe, passing it over as though it was unimportant. Possibly he intended to use it elsewhere and preferred not to dilute it by telling the story twice. However, it is such a well-known tale that it is necessary to include it. Consequently the story is fleshed out by using the legend recorded by his contemporary and bitter opponent, Matilda Coxe Stevenson, whose work is based on an indivisible mixture of both her's and her husband's field research. The tale, however, belongs to Cushing's era. A certain amount of license has been incorporated into this oft-told tale with regard to the wet bowstring event which has been attributed first to the Zuni and then the Kianakwe, varying with the individual telling the tale.

The Kianakwe ceremony was formerly presented every four years by the Zuni (Wright 1985, 74), lasting well into this century, and may still be presented if the proper ceremonialists are living and have the desire. The myth either explains anomalies in Zuni social organization, or the elements represented in their ceremonial practices are the surviving fragments of an actual historical event. There is a Black Corn segment of the Zuni Corn clan who gives special attention to the impersonation of the Chákwaina Ókya during the Winter Solstice ceremonies. The dance of the Kianakwe is marked by several peculiarities. First, it is a round dance, a form alien to Zuni kachina performances but typical of Hopi women's dances. Secondly it is a give-away dance, again like the Hopi women's dances. Thirdly it always includes three kachinas other than the Kianakwe who are: Saíyathlia, one of the Koyemshi, and Kothlamana. The dance is accompanied by giving of quantities of food to the elders of the midmost kiva, much in the manner of giving tribute. Finally, when the Kianakwe leave they do not go to Kóthluwalawan but instead leave to the south.

Notes: 23 The Clans Divide in Their Search for the Middle

The myths of the Pueblo Indians are filled with epics of movement, migration legends, stories of wandering about over the face of the land. Although it seems a contradiction in terms to have nomadic villages, nevertheless that was the native pattern of existence prior to the Spanish Entrada. Villages were built and fields planted, then after a few decades the towns were abandoned and the people moved on, nomads in slow motion. Why they moved almost certainly has as many answers as there are abandoned sites. The Pueblo Indians advance their reasons in their migration myths while archaeologists state theirs in terms of drought, famine, warfare, disease, and various forms of social unrest.

The migration myth, as the story of such wanderings and the reasons for it, satisfies the native belief but does not lend itself to accurate historical reconstruction. That the stories cannot be taken at face value was demonstrated by J.W. Fewkes in his continuing but unsuccessful efforts to trace Hopi movements through their legends. However, such movements did take place and are often substantiated by archaeological excavations as well as social and historical evidence.

In the migrations narrated by the Zuni of today in their ceremonials, there is evidence of borrowing from the Keresans to the north of societies like the Shumakwe and other curing fraternities (Parsons 1939, 134–5, 876 N.★, 969). But when

149

this occurred is another matter. As an example, legend of movement through the middle region has additional support in the similarities that exist in pottery designs from Mátsaki village at Zuni, the Hopi town of Awatovi, and Pottery Mound on the Rio Puerco of the east, as well as in the mural paintings of the latter two villages (Hibben 1975; Smith 1952). Migration routes in the Southwest are in an incipient stage of understanding with one route being championed by a set of scientists and just as fiercely argued by another set as the bare bones of history emerge for that region. Whether the Zuni are explaining the presence of round villages adjoining square ones as they exist today in nearby canyons, or whether the migration legend of the southern clans is based on fact, is a moot question until archaeological excavations produce hard data to uphold the grain of truth in the native versions.

Notes: 24 The Council of Men and Beings

The water skate, family Gerridae, is found throughout the Southwest on almost every body of water. These small insects scavenge the surface of the water, supported by its surface tension. They are noted by research biologists for their extreme nervousness which makes them a poor addition to any aquarium. They cluster in swarms, bobbing up and down, then race away at any disturbance. Because of this timid behavior they are known to many native-Americans as water deer.

Although the body shape appears to be a four-legged linear form, two other legs, pointing forward, lie along the body and are not noticeable. Cushing consistently speaks of the water skate as a six-legged creature and consequently a being

that should be associated with the six directions. In this myth the vertical dimensions of up and down are unneeded but Cushing must have presumed that since it was an insect all six legs would be used. The water skate does not occur in legends with the frequency of the dragonflies. Dragonflies are most often portrayed on altars, pottery, and petroglyphs, possibly because they are shamanistic creatures (Parsons 1926, 250) and have supernatural powers (Benedict 1935, v.II, 9) whereas the water skate is not so considered. The image of the water skate does appear frequently on the back of kachina masks and as a petroglyph where it is frequently mistaken for a lizard.

It is quite likely that the water skate (above) was chosen for the task of locating the Middle as much for its affinity to water as for its directional shape. Certainly its habit of raising and lowering its body fits well with the story.

Notes: 25 Corn Mountain and the Great Flood

Cushing chose to pass lightly over the story of the great flood and the flight of the Zuni to Dówa Yálanne just as he did the tale of the Kianakwe. His account mentions the sacrificed boy and girl only after the fact and fails to mention the Great Water Serpent, Ko'loowisi, at all. Consequently the legend recorded by his inimical rival, Matilda Coxe Stevenson, has been used (Stevenson 1904, 61).

The Water Serpent is a collective being who may be found in every spring or body of water (Parsons 1939, 184). Although there are variations in form, the commonest is the Plumed Water Serpent, present throughout the Pueblo World. These beings are the cause of earthquakes, floods, and landslides (ibid., 1017). Careless approach to springs can cause a fatal swelling of the abdomen, particularly in young men. Even the paint from the serpent's image can produce a similar result. If young women immerse themselves in a spring they run the risk of becoming impregnated by the Water Serpent.

Like the Maya and Aztec who conceived of ritual drowning, the Puebloans occasionally sacrificed a young boy or girl to ward off disaster (ibid., 1017 N.‡) but were never profligate in their use of human life. At Zuni such sacrifice was used to stop the flood waters. Undoubtedly the great flood was the one that buried Halónawan. However, with the accretion of tales from Christianity, the immensity of the biblical flood became incorporated to make it reach the tops of the surrounding mountains. The fact that Corn Mountain was occupied to avoid Spanish retribution is conveniently forgotten. With etiological reasoning the two monumentally distinctive pillars that jut from the west side of Dówa Yálanne become the sacrificial boy and girl watching forever over Zuni.

Sources of the Myths

1. Genesis:
   The Genesis of the Worlds, or the Beginning of the Newness.
   The Genesis of Men and Creatures.
   [Cushing 1896, 379–80]
2. Formation of the Worlds:
   The Genesis of Men and the Creatures.
   [ibid., 380–81]
3. Birth of the Twins:
   The Birth from the Sea of the Twain Deliverers of Men.
   [ibid., 381–82]
4. The First World:
   The Birth and Delivery of Men and the Creatures.
   [ibid., 382–83]
5. The Daylight World:
   The Condition of Men When First into the World of Daylight Born.
   The Origin of Priests and Knowledge.
   [ibid., 383–84]

6. The Winter and Summer People:
   The Origin of the Raven and the Macaw, Totems of Winter and Summer.
   [ibid., 384–86]
7. The Origins of Clans and Societies:
   The Origin and Naming of Totem-Clans and Creature Kinds, and the
     Division and Naming of Spaces and Things.
   The Origin of the Councils of Secrecy or Sacred Brotherhoods.
   [ibid., 386–88]
8. The Hardening of the World:
   The Unripeness and Instability of the World When Still Young.
   The Hardening of the World and the First Settlements of Men.
   The Beginning of the Search for the Middle of the World, and the Second
     Tarrying of Men.
   The Learning of War and the Third Tarrying.
   [ibid., 388–390]
9. The Meeting of the Seed Peoples:
   The Meeting of the People of the Dew, and the Fourth Tarrying.
   The Generation of the Seed of Seeds or the Origin of Corn.
   [ibid., 390–91]
10. The First-Growing-Grass Clan:
   The Generation of the Seed of Seeds or the Origin of Corn.
   [ibid., 391–93]
11. The People of the Dew:
   The Generation of the Seed of Seeds or the Origin of Corn.
   [ibid., 393–95]
12. The Blessing of the Deities:
   The Generation of the Seed of Seeds or the Origin of Corn.
   [ibid., 395–98]
13. The Search for the Middle:
   The Renewal of the Search for the Middle.
   The Choosing of Seekers for Signs of the Middle.
   The Change-Making Sin of the Brother and Sister.
   The Birth of the Old Ones or Ancients of the Kâ'kâ.
   [ibid., 398–401]
14. The Separation of the Clans:
   The Renewal of the Great Journey, and the Sundering of the Tribes of Men.
   [ibid., 403–04]
15. The Abode of Souls:
   The Origin of Death by Dying, and the Abode of Souls and the Kâ'kâ.
   The Loss of the Great Southern Clans.
   The Saving of the Father-Clans.
   The Awaiting of the Lost Clans.
   [ibid., 404–06]

16. The Journeys of Kiaḳlo:
    The Straying of K'yäk'lu and His Plaint to the Waterfowl.
    How the Duck, Hearing, Was Fain to Guide K'yäk'lu.
    How the Rainbow Worm Bore K'yäk'lu to the Plain of Kâ''hluëlane.
    The Tarrying of K'yäk'lu in the Plain and His Dismay.
    [ibid., 406–09]
17. Kiaḳlo and the Council of the Gods:
    How the Duck Found the Lake of the Dead and the Gods of the Kâ'kâ.
    How the Gods of the Kâ'kâ Counselled the Duck.
    How by Behest of the Duck the Kâ'yemäshi Sought K'yäk'lu to Convey Him
        to the Lake of the Dead.
    How the Kâ'yemäshi Bore K'yäk'lu to the Council of the Gods.
    The Council of the Kâ'kâ, and the Instruction of K'yäk'lu by the Gods.
    [ibid., 409–13]
18. How Kiaḳlo Came to His People:
    The Instruction of the Kâ'yemäshi by K'yäk'lu.
    How the Kâ'yemäshi Bore K'yäk'lu to His People.
    The Return of K'yäk'lu and His Sacred Instructions to the People.
    The Enjoining of the K'yäk'lu Ámosi, and the Departure of K'yäk'lu and the
        Old-Ones.
    [ibid., 413–14]
19. The Return of the Brothers Ánahoho:
    The Coming of the Brothers Ánahoho and the Runners of the Kâ'Kâ.
    The Dispatching of the Souls of Things to the Souls of the Dead.
    [ibid., 414–15]
20. The Great Journey Renewed:
    The Renewal of the Great Journeying and of the Search for the Middle.
    The Warning Speech of the Gods, and the Untailing of Men.
    [ibid., 415–17]
21. The Twin War Gods and the Origin of the Priests of the Bow:
    The Origin of the Twin Gods of War and of the Priesthood of the Bow.
    [ibid., 417–24]
22. War with the Black People:
    The Downfall of Hán'hlipíŋk'ya, and the Search Anew for the Middle.
    The Wars with the Black People of the High Buildings, and with the
        Ancient Woman of the K'ya'kweina and Other Kâ'kâkwe.
    The Adoption of the Black People, and the Division of the Clans to Search
        for the Middle.
    [ibid., 424–25]
    Destruction of the Kĭa'nakwe, and Songs of Thanksgiving.
    [Stevenson 1904, 36–38]
23. The Clans Divide in Their Search for the Middle:
    The Adoption of the Black People, and the Division of the Clans to Search
        for the Middle.

The Northward Eastern Journey of the Winter Clans.

The Southward Eastern Journey of the Summer Clans.

The Eastward Middle Journey of the People of the Middle.

The Settlement of Zuni-land and the Building of the Seven Great Towns Therein.

The Reunion of the People of the Middle with the Summer and Seed People.

[Cushing 1896, 425–28]

24. The Great Council of Men and Beings:

The Great Council of Men and the Beings for the Determination of the True Middle.

The Establishment of the Fathers and Their Tabernacle at Hálonawan or the Erring-Place of the Middle.

[ibid., 428–29]

25. Corn Mountain and the Great Flood:

The Flooding of the Towns and the Building of the City of Seed on the Mountain.

The Staying of the Flood by Sacrifice of the Youth and the Maiden, and the Establishment of Hálona Ítiwana on the True Middle.

The Custom of Testing the Middle in the Middle Time.

[ibid., 429–30]

The Flight of the Áshiwi To To'wa Yäl'länně and Their Return to the Valley.

[Stevenson 1904, 61]

Glossary

Áchiakiakwe: The Makers and Defenders of Pathways. The Great Knife Society of Zuni.

Áhaiyuta: The Two War Gods or the Elder of the Two War Gods. He is also called Ko'witúma and Uyuyewi.

Aik'yako-kwe: The First-Growing-Grass People.

Ákakakwe: The People of Acoma.

Ána: Ouch!

Ánahoho: Kiaḱlo's two brothers who went south in search of the Middle.

Ánahoho áchi: The younger brothers of Kiaḱlo.

Ánosin Téhuli: The first or Soot World.

Ápoyan Ta'chu: The Sky Father.

Áshiwi: The Zuni's name for themselves.

Awatovi: A large Hopi town destroyed in 1703 by internecine warfare.

Áwisho Téhuli: The third or Mud World.

Áwitelin Tsíta: The Earth Mother.

Áwonawílona: The Maker or Container of All, the All-Father.

Bitsitsi: The personage representing

Paíyatuma during the ceremony of the return of the Corn Maidens.

Chákwaina Ókyatsiki: The Ancient Warrior Woman of the Kianakwe.

Chamahia: A ceremonial stone celt formerly used in war.

Chipía: An ancient mythological city in the Sandia Mountains.

Chúetone: A germinal fetish believed to produce plant seeds.

Dówa Yálanne: Corn Mountain, a large mesa immediately east of the Pueblo of Zuni.

Halóna: The present-day town of Zuni.

Halóna Ítiwana: The Middle Ant Heap of the World. Present-day Zuni.

Halónawan: The portion of Zuni immediately south of the Zuni River. Occupied prehistorically.

Hámpasawan: One of the seven Zuni cities present in 1600 A.D.

Hán'thlipíngkia: The Place of Sacred Stealing. Where the Zuni had their tails removed. Origin place of the Priests of the Bow.

Hápanawan: Abode of the ghosts.

Ha'thl'tunkia: Storm Chief of the North.

Hátin-kiaiakwi: Listening Spring.

Háwikuh: One of the seven Zuni cities present in 1600 A.D.

Héhea: The timid runner kachina of the gods.

Hékwainankwin: The settlement near the mud springs on the banks of the Rio Puerco of the West.

Héshotatsína: The Town of Speech Markings in the south [Town of Petroglyphs].

Huruing Wuhti: The Hopi deity of Hard Substances.

Ítsepasha: The Game-Making Koyemshi. The Glum One captured by the Kianakwe.

Iwaiyahuna: Kiaklo's personal name used by the Koyemshi.

Jimit'kianap-kiatea: The spring where the Zuni emerged from the Underworlds.

Ka'ka: Either kachinas or ravens.

Ka'kakwe: Either the Raven People or the Black People.

Ka'wimosa: The Kachina Maker. Kiaklo's father, a Rain Priest.

Ke'tchina: One of the seven Zuni cities present in 1600 A.D.

K'éyatiwanki: The Place of Raised Land.

Kiaklo: Páutiwa's Speaker. Ka'wimosa's oldest son. The keeper of Zuni history.

Kianakwe: The white-robed people who fought against the Zuni.

Kíwitsin: The kiva of the kachinas.

Kókokshi: The Dance of Good. The first kachinas or Beautiful Dancers.

Kokyang Wuhti: The Spider Grandmother, a deity of the Hopi.

Ko'loowisi: The Plumed Water Serpent.

K'ólin Téhuli: The second or Moss World.

Kopishtaiya: Keresan supernaturals.

Kothlamana: The Man-Woman Kachina. The first born of Síweluhsiwa and Síwiluhsitsa. Elder sister of the Koyemshi.

Kóthluwalanne: The area where Kóthluwalawan is located.

Kóthluwalawan: The Great City of the Kachinas in the Lake of Whispering Waters.

Ko'wituma: The elder of the Twin Gods before their change.

Koyemshi: The caretakers or husbands of the kachinas. The offspring of incest between Síweluhsiwa and Síwiluhsitsa.

Kúyapalitsa: The personal name of the Chákwaina Ókyatsiki.

Kwa'kina: One of the seven Zuni cities present in 1600 A.D. The origin place of the Brotherhood of Fire [Mákekwe] and the Mountain Sheep Dance.

Kwélele: The God of Flame. The Black Kachina.

Kwínikwakwe: The Kianakwe or the Black People. Enemies of the Zuni.

K'yáetone: The germinal fetish believed to produce water and rain.

Kyakime: One of the seven Zuni cities present in 1600 A.D.

K'yanas'tipe: The Water Skater.

K'yánawe: One of the seven Zuni cities present in 1600 A.D.

Mákekwe: The Brotherhood of Fire. A curing society.

Malachpeta: The Finger-marked Kachina of the Hopi.

Mamzrau: A Hopi Woman's Society.

Marau: Hopi Woman's Society dance.

Masau-u: The Hopi Deity of the Underworld, Death, and Fire.

Mátsailema: The personal name of the younger War God Twin. Referred to as one of the Áhaiyuta he is also called Wats'usi.

Mátsaki: One of the seven Zuni cities present in 1600 A.D. The Zuni believed it was near "the Middle". The place where the Macaw People met the People of the Seed.

Matya: A Hopi kachina. The name means "pressed against", referring to the handprint marked on the face.

Móyachun Thlánna: The Great Morning Star.

Mú'etone: The germinal fetish believed to produce hail and soil.

Múlakwe: The Macaw People.

Nahoydadatsia: A Hopi game consisting of a ball tethered to a short stick that is hit according to very complicated rules.

Néwekwe: The Society or Brotherhood of Medicine and Magic.

Ohewa: The eastern kiva at Zuni.

Óloma: The Storm Chief of the South.

Pachaiyanpi: The sieve or rain wheel of the Hopi.

Paíyatuma: The Deity of Morning, Flutes, Youth, and Dew.

Palhik'o Mana: The Hopi Rain-Drinking Girl. A part of the Mamzrau ceremony.

Páutiwa: The Sun Priest of Souls, the Cloud Sender. Chief of the kachinas.

Pekwin: A speaker chief.

Pialawe: A miniature shield used as a prayer object.

Póshaiyangki: The Master Curer from the Northeast.

Saishíwani: The Storm Chief of the Nadir.

Saíyathlia: The Warrior God. The initiator of youths. A kachina.

Sálimopia: Warriors of the Six Directions.

Sániakiakwe: The Society or Brotherhood of Hunters.

Saushúlima: The Storm Chief of the Zenith.

Shalako: Six giant kachinas called Couriers of the Gods.

Shípap: The Keresan term for Shípapolima.

Shípapolima: The mythical city of the mists.

Shípololon K'yaía: The Place of Steam Mist Rising from the Waters.

Shi'tsukia: The White Kachina. Kwélele's partner during the Winter

Solstice ceremonies. Páutiwa's son-in-law.

Shíwanakwe: The Society or Brotherhood of Priests. A Rain Society.

Shiwanna: A rain priest.

Shiwína Téu'thlkwaina: The upper valley of the Zuni River.

Shiwína Yálawan: The Zuni Mountains.

Shókoniman: Home of the flute-canes in the south.

Shóko Yálanne: Mountain of the flute-canes. Sierra Escudilla.

Shómitakia: The song used to call forth all the Chiefs of Directions.

Shúlawitsi: The Little Fire God.

Shumakwe: A society at Zuni that cures lameness and blindness.

Sipapu: The place where the Hopi emerged from the Underworld.

Sivu-i-qiltaka: The Hopi Pot-Carrier Kachina.

Síweluhsiwa: The son of Ka'wimosa and the father of the Koyemshi.

Síwíluhsitsa: The daughter of Ka'wimosa and the mother of the Koyemshi.

Támelan K'yaíyawan: The Place Where the Trees Stood in Water.

Ta'iya: The Place of Planting. Las Nutrias.

Tawa: The Hopi Sun God.

Téhuli: Womb or cave.

Glossary

Téhulikwin: A dark enclosed inside space.

Ték'ohaian Úlahnane: The fifth or Daylight World.

Ténatsali: The Deity of Time and Directions. A Medicine flower. Cushing's Zuni name.

Tépahaian Téhuli: The fourth or Wing World.

Tésak'ya Yala: The Place of Bare Mountains.

Thla'hewe: The Corn Dance or ceremony.

Thlétokwe: The Brotherhood or Wood Society.

Tsaí'luh'tsanokia: The Storm Chief of the East.

Tulakin Mana: The Hopi Stirring Girl Kachina who accompanies the Pot-Carrying Kachina.

Uheponolo: The Storm Chief of the West.

Úk'yawane: Snow Water River. The Rio Puerco of the West.

Únahsinte: The Storm Chief of All Directions or the Middle.

Uwannami: Rain spirits.

Úyuyewi: The personal name of the elder War God Twin.

Wats'usi: The personal name of the younger of the Twin Gods before their change.

Wenima: An archaic or Keresan name for Kóthluwalawan.

Yála Tétsinapa: The Mountain of Space Markings.

Yaná-uluha: The first Rain Priest and Speaker of the Sun. The Beginner of the Priesthood. The Leader of the Priests.

Yápot-uluha: Foster child of Yaná-uluha. Member of the Water clan. Father of the Corn.

Yatoka: The Sun Father.

In an effort to reduce the difficulty of reading Cushing's and Stevenson's complex orthography, the Zuni words have been reduced to a phoneticized spelling that retains only the accent ´ and the glottal stop '. In most instances the early orthography does not agree with the currently accepted spellings of the Zuni tribe. In addition, the more commonly known words of kiva and kachina have been substituted for kiwitsin and koko or kâkâ.

Bibliography

Benedict, Ruth
1935   *Zuni Mythology*. Columbia University Contributions to
            Anthropology, Vol. XXI 1 & 2. New York: Columbia University
            Press.
Bunzel, Ruth L.
1932a   *Introduction to Zuni Ceremonialism*. Forty-seventh Annual Report of
            the Bureau of American Ethnology 1929–1930, pp. 467–544.
            Washington, D.C.
1932b   *Zuni Kachinas: An Analytical Study*. Forty-seventh Annual Report
            of the Bureau of American Ethnology 1929–1930, pp. 837–1086.
            Washington, D.C.
1933   *Zuni Texts*. American Ethnological Society Publications, Vol. XV.
            New York.
Colton, Harold S.
1959   *Hopi Kachina Dolls*. Albuquerque: University of New Mexico
            Press.
Courlander, Harold
1971   *The Fourth World of the Hopis*. New York: Crown Publishers, Inc.

Cushing, Frank Hamilton

1882–83   *My Adventures in Zuni.* Century Illustrated Monthly Magazine.
          Reprint: Palo Alto: American West Publishing Company 1970.

1883   *Zuni Fetiches.* Second Annual Report of the Bureau of American
          Ethnology 1880–1881, pp. 9–45. Washington, D.C.

1892   *A Zuni Folktale of the Underworld.* Journal of American Folk-Lore,
          Vol. V No. 2, pp. 49–56.

1896   *Outlines of Zuni Creation Myths.* Thirteenth Annual Report of the
          Bureau of American Ethnology 1891–92, pp. 321–447. Washington,
          D.C.

1920   *Zuni Breadstuff.* Indian Notes and Monographs, Vol. VIII,
          Museum of the American Indian. New York: Heye Foundation.

1923   *Origin Myth from Oraibi.* Journal of American Folk-Lore, Vol.
          XXXVI, pp. 163–70.

1979   *Zuni, Selected Writings of Frank Hamilton Cushing.* Edited by Jesse
          Green. Lincoln, Nebr.: University of Nebraska Press.

Eggan, Fred

1950   *Social Organization of the Western Pueblos.* Chicago: The University
          of Chicago Press.

Fewkes, Jesse Walter

1892   *A Few Summer Ceremonials at the Tusayan Pueblos.* Journal of
          American Ethnology and Archaeology, Vol. II, Pt.1. New York.

Franciscan Fathers

1910   *An Ethnologic Dictionary of the Navaho Language.* St. Michaels,
          Ariz.: Franciscan Fathers.

Hibben, Frank C.

1975   *Kiva Art of the Anasazi at Pottery Mound.* Las Vegas. KC
          Publications.

Hodge, F.W.

1937   *History of Hawikuh, New Mexico, One of the So-called Cities of
          Cibola.* Publications of the F.W. Hodge Anniversary Fund, Vol. 1.
          Highland Park, Calif.: Southwest Museum.

Hough, Walter

1914   *The Culture of the Ancient Pueblos of the Upper Gila Region, New
          Mexico and Arizona.* Smithsonian Institution Bulletin No. 87.
          Washington, D.C.: United States National Museum.

Ortiz, Alfonso

1969   *The Tewa World.* Chicago: The University of Chicago Press.

Parsons, Elsie Clews

1917   *Notes on Zuni.* Memoirs, Vol. IV No. 4 pt. 2. Lancaster, Penn.:
          American Anthropological Association.

1925   *The Pueblo of Jemez.* Papers of the Southwestern Expedition No. 3.
          Andover, Mass.: Phillips Academy.

1926   *Tewa Tales.* Memoirs of the American Folk-Lore Society, Vol. XIX. New York.

1939   *Pueblo Indian Religion.* Vols. 1 & 2. Chicago: The University of Chicago Press.

Smith, Watson

1952   *Kiva Mural Decorations at Awatovi and Kawaika. with a survey of other wall paintings in the Pueblo Southwest.* Papers of the Peabody Museum of American Archaeology & Ethnology, Harvard University. Volume XXXVII. Cambridge, Mass. Published by Peabody Museum.

Stephen, Alexander M.

1929   *Hopi Tales.* Journal of American Folk-Lore, Vol. XLII, pp. 1–72.

1936   *Hopi Journal of Alexander M. Stephen.* Edited by Elsie Clews Parson. Contributions to Anthropology, Vol. 23 1 & 2. New York: Columbia University Press.

Stevenson, Matilda Coxe

1894   *The Sia.* Eleventh Annual Report of the Bureau of American Ethnology 1889–1890, pp. 9–157. Washington, D.C.

1904   *The Zuni Indians.* Twenty-third Annual Report of the Bureau of American Ethnology 1901–1902. Washington, D.C.

Titiev, Mischa

1944   *Old Oraibi: A Study of the Hopi Indians of Third Mesa.* Papers of the Peabody Museum of American Archaeology and Ethnology, Vol. XXII No. 1. Cambridge, Mass.: Peabody Museum.

Voth, H.R.

1905   *The Traditions of the Hopi.* Field Columbian Museum Publication 96, Anthropological Series, Vol. VIII. Chicago.

1912   *The Oraibi Marau Ceremony.* Field Museum of Natural History Publication 156, Anthropological Series, Vol. XI No.1. Chicago.

White, Leslie A.

1932   *The Acoma Indians.* Forty-seventh Annual Report of the Bureau of American Ethnology 1929–1930, pp. 17–192. Washington, D.C.

1962   *The Pueblo of Sia, New Mexico.* Bureau of American Ethnology, Bul. 184. Smithsonian Institution: Washington, D.C.

Wright, Barton

1985   *Kachinas of the Zuni.* Flagstaff, Ariz.: Northland Press.

Zim, Herbert S. and Baker, Robert H.

1956   *Stars, a Guide to the Constellations, Sun, Moon, Planets, and other Features of the Heavens.* New York: Simon and Schuster.